WOE IS I JR.

WOE IS **I** JR.

THE YOUNGER GRAMMARPHOBE'S GUIDE TO BETTER ENGLISH

in Plain English

Patricia T. O'Conner

DRAWINGS BY
Tom Stiglich

G. P. PUTNAM'S SONS

G. P. PUTNAM'S SONS
A division of Penguin Young Readers Group.
Published by The Penguin Group.
Penguin Group (USA) Inc., 375 Hudson Street, New York, NY 10014, U.S.A.
Penguin Group (Canada), 90 Eglinton Avenue East, Suite 700, Toronto, Ontario, Canada M4P 2Y3
(a division of Pearson Penguin Canada Inc.).
Penguin Books Ltd, 80 Strand, London WC2R 0RL, England.
Penguin Ireland, 25 St. Stephen's Green, Dublin 2, Ireland
(a division of Penguin Books Ltd.).
Penguin Group (Australia), 250 Camberwell Road, Camberwell, Victoria 3124,
Australia (a division of Pearson Australia Group Pty Ltd).
Penguin Books India Pvt Ltd, 11 Community Centre, Panchsheel Park,
New Delhi - 110 017, India.
Penguin Group (NZ), 17 Apollo Drive, Mairangi Bay, Auckland 1311,
New Zealand (a division of Pearson New Zealand Ltd).
Penguin Books (South Africa) (Pty) Ltd, 24 Sturdee Avenue, Rosebank,
Johannesburg 2196, South Africa.
Penguin Books Ltd, Registered Offices: 80 Strand, London WC2R 0RL, England.

Published simultaneously in Canada. Printed in the United States of America.
Design by Marikka Tamura. Text set in Berthold Baskerville.
Library of Congress Cataloging-in-Publication Data
O'Conner, Patricia T. Woe is I jr. : the younger grammarphobe's guide to
better English in plain English / Patricia T. O'Conner; illustrations by Tom Stiglich. p. cm.
Includes index. 1. English language–Grammar–Juvenile literature. 2. English language–Usage–
Juvenile literature. I. Title. PE1112.O277 2007 372.6'1–dc22 2006020575
ISBN 978-0-399-24331-8
1 3 5 7 9 10 8 6 4 2
First Impression

For my sister, Kathy Richard

CONTENTS

ACKNOWLEDGMENTS
WOE IS I
JR.

A book like this one is impossible to do all by yourself. Fortunately, I didn't have to. So many kind people, children as well as grown-ups, helped in so many ways that it's more of a group effort than the work of a single author.

Librarians, teachers, and school administrators were generous with their advice and guidance. I'm grateful to Valerie Annis, Beverly Backstrom, Suzanne Burley, Cathy Colella, Jeffrey Phillips, Michelle Segerson, Erin Simmons, and Gloria Urban. Special thanks must go to a special teacher, Keri Snowden, and to her fifth-grade class at the Booth Free School in Roxbury, Connecticut.

It's been a long time since I was in the middle grades myself, but luckily lots of people were able to refresh my memory about the kid's point of view.

Two awesome girls, Emma Gordon and Mady Sheets, were especially helpful. And many more children graciously shared their thoughts on all kinds of things. Thank you, Sydney Alworth, Thomas Andrews, Samantha Bisignano, Katherine Bradley, Richard Bradley, Travis Bresson, Ashley Brolin-Dirienzo, Stephen Cangelosi, Julia Coyle, Cornel David, Jessica Dumas, James "J.J." Einbinder, Anthony Graziani, Becky Hamilton, Emmy Hamilton, Grace Kellogg, Sam Kratzer, Zach Krin, Chris Lowe, Christina Loya, Bridget McCarthy, Emily Morris, Kirby Peters, Ben Steers, Will Stuart, Rachel Vallerie, Cassidy Westervelt, and Richie Wilhelm.

There would be no books without publishers and editors. I'm particularly indebted to three savvy women: Jane Isay, who persuaded me years ago to write the original *Woe Is I*; Susan Kochan at Putnam, who suggested that children might like their own version of the book; and Anna Jardine, copy editor extraordinaire. If any errors remain, they're mine alone.

My agent, Dan Green, and my friend Peggy Richards read the manuscript and offered helpful comments. It's great to have people on your side, but it's even better when they're terribly, terribly smart. And speaking of smart, thank you, Merrill Perlman, David Kelly, and Charles Doherty. I owe you!

My biggest debt of all, however, is to my writing colleague, chief editor, husband, and best friend, Stewart Kellerman, whose intelligence and good sense are reflected on every page. This book appears under my name alone, but it's a product of a line-by-line, word-by-word partnership in which my thoughts and his go hand in hand.

INTRODUCTION
WOE IS I JR.

In case you're wondering what a grammarphobe is, I'll end the suspense. It's somebody who has a phobia, or fear, about grammar. This phobia is extremely common. That's why there are so many grammarphobes around, and why they come in all shapes and sizes. If you're one of the shorter ones, this book is for you.

Before we get started, though, let's leave our phobias behind.

Contrary to popular opinion, grammar isn't gruesome. Neither is it ghastly or gross or grim. Actually, grammar isn't growly in the least.

Grammarphobes have the impression that grammar is some kind of ordeal. If that's what you think, you've been misinformed. Torture is entirely unnecessary, and it's almost never used to teach grammar these days. Besides, the tools needed—the thumbscrews, the rack, the cat-o'-nine-tails—are hard to find, even on eBay.

So torture is out. I know you're disappointed, but you'll have plenty of opportunities to suffer later in life. Wait till you have to work for a living.

The truth is that grammar can be fun. You like telling and hearing stories, don't you? Joking with your friends and sharing the latest news? E-mailing and instant-messaging? What makes it all possible is grammar, the art of putting words together to make sentences. You use grammar even when you talk to your pets, who sometimes listen and sometimes don't. In fact, you use grammar every time you use words to get an idea across. You do this all the time, putting particular words in a particular order, sometimes without even thinking.

So why think about it? Because good grammar helps you get the right idea across. If your words aren't right, or if they're not in the right order, the person you're talking to might get the wrong idea. This can have dire consequences.

I'll illustrate my point with what I call the Bad News Rule. Here's how it works. You learn that your friend Chip has fallen off his skateboard and broken his arm. You send him an instant message: "I heard you're bad news."

Oops! You meant to say the news was bad. But you've actually said that Chip is bad news! You wrote *you're*—a word that's short for "you are"—when you should have used *your*. The result? Instead of sympathy, you've sent an insult. Now, that's bad news. Sure, you meant well. But what gets through is what counts.

Grammar helps us understand each other. Think of it as an owner's manual for assembling the words in your head. You have to put your words together the right way if you want them to make sense to somebody else. They won't do what you want if they aren't assembled correctly.

What if every kid you know had a different owner's manual? How would you agree on what your words meant or how to assemble them? You might as well be speaking different languages. Imagine two friends playing cards. If one of them thinks the game is Hearts and the other thinks it's Crazy Eights, they won't have much of a game. (Anybody for Fifty-two Pick-up?)

Communicating is a lot like playing cards. To make sense, we have to play the same game, and by the same rules. So what are the rules for playing the game of English? You already know most of them without having to open a book.

Take the words *slobber* and *slobbered*, for instance. You use them to talk about the same activity (slobbering), but on different occasions. *Little Maggie* **slobbered** *yesterday and she* **will slobber** *tomorrow.*

Another example is *I* and *me.* You use them to refer to the same person (yourself), but in different situations. *I am about to explode! Don't mess with **me!***

Another is *tarantula* and *tarantulas.* You use them to talk about the same creature (a large, hairy spider with a nasty bite), but in different quantities. *Bart sat on a **tarantula**! Lisa sat on three **tarantulas**!*

Choices, choices! You can see why we need some rules. Without them, things could get pretty confusing. How would we say *when* Maggie slobbered, *who* is about to explode, or *how many* tarantulas got squished?

Nobody's perfect, of course. Some very smart people mess up *I* and *me.* Others can't spell. Lots of people don't know the difference between *it's* and *its.* Some go out of their way to avoid using quotation marks. Whatever your particular boo-boo, *Woe Is I Jr.* can set you straight without resorting to instruments of torture.

But why a book? Why not use the grammar-checker in your computer? I'm glad you asked. Grammar-checkers suck. If yours is anything like mine, and it probably is, many of the "mistakes" it catches aren't really mistakes at all. Guess whose job it is to check the grammar-checker's grammar?

Before you have an anxiety attack, though, I'll let you in on a secret: English is fun and quirky and interesting. Why? Because it's supersized and has soaked up words from nearly every other language you can think of: French, Italian, Spanish, German, Arabic, Dutch, Chinese, Portuguese, Japanese, Yiddish, Persian, Greek, Latin, and many more. And it hasn't stopped. It's a work in progress, with plenty of room for new words and new ways of saying things.

Although words and phrases come and go, the underlying rules of English usually stay the same. But even they can occasionally change. Here's what I mean. Once upon a time, a knock-knock joke would have started like this.

"Knock, knock."

"Who's there?"

"It is I."

Nowadays, of course, most people say, "It's *me*," or "It is *me*." We no longer believe that *is* must always be followed by *I* instead of *me*. If you want to sound like the Queen of England, go ahead and say, "It is *I*." You're allowed, but you don't have to.

You probably know where this is leading. Why did I call my book *Woe Is I*, when anybody in her right mind would have chosen *Woe Is Me*, even the Queen of England? Well, I wanted to show how ridiculous we sound when we try too hard to be "correct." That's what grammarphobia does to people. It makes them a little crazy.

The original *Woe Is I* was meant for grown-up grammarphobes, but kids said they found it useful, too—or some of it, anyway. This new version of the book concentrates on that "some of it." And that's about the sum of it!

CHAPTER 1

"I" WITNESS
When Words Need Stand-ins

Before you knew any words at all, you had to point and grunt to communicate. Pointing and grunting is OK when you're a baby, but after a while people expect you to use words. (Of course, even grown-ups sometimes point and grunt. Maybe your dad does at the dinner table, though—you hope—not in public.)

Luckily, using words is not difficult. As you've probably found out, there are words for just about everything. If something needs to be discussed, you can bet there's a word for it. There are even words for things that you're not supposed to mention. (Let's not mention them!) Every time something new comes along, along comes the appropriate word. This is very convenient. Grunting is almost never necessary.

You don't have to know the name of something in order to talk about it, though. That's why the word *it* was invented (or *they*, if you're talking about more than one something). The same goes for *he, she, we, I, you,* and other substitute words that stand in for real names.

Take for example that fat, puffy thing you're sitting on. (No, not your butt! The beanbag chair, silly.) You can use its real name: *beanbag.* You can say, "The *beanbag* is lumpy." Or you can take a shortcut and use a teeny-weeny stand-in: "*It* is lumpy."

The real name, *beanbag,* is what a grammar teacher would call a noun. A noun is a word for a person, a place, or a thing. The stand-in, *it,* is called a pronoun (*pro* means "for"). So a pronoun is a stand-in for a noun.

Don't worry. In real life you hardly ever need to use grammatical terms like "noun" and "pronoun." But I'm including them in case you'd like to impress your parents by sprinkling them into your conversation.

("Great choice of pronoun, Dad!") Meanwhile, since pronouns are substitutes for real names, just think of them as stand-ins.

THE NAME GAME

Stand-ins are easy to recognize. There are lots of them, but they're so small that you could fit them all in a lunch box. You know them already, because you use them every day. Who, me? Yes, you!

Let's pretend your name is Sam. It might be Samuel, or Samantha, or plain old Sam. You decide. This is only temporary.

Now, pretend the mayor of your town has outlawed the words *I*, *me*, and *my*. (The mayor has lost a few marbles. This, too, is only temporary.)

Just try talking without using the words *I*, *me*, and *my*. What happens? Every time you say anything about yourself, you have to use your name. This means you repeat yourself a lot.

You can't say, "*I* am furious." You have to say, "Sam is furious."

You can't say, "Please pass *me* the salt." You have to say, "Please pass Sam the salt."

And you can't say, "Hello, *my* name is Sam." You have to say, "Hello, Sam's name is Sam." Strange, but true!

Of course, instead of "Sam" you might say "this person now talking to you," or point to yourself (which would be rude), or hold up a recent photo. But you get the picture. *I*, *me*, and *my* are handy words to have around.

They and their cousins (*we*, *us*, *he*, *she*, *him*, *her*, *it*, *they*, *them*, and more) are examples of stand-ins. So *he* or *him* can stand in for "my older brother, Wilbur." *She* or *her* can take the place of "my three-year-old sister, Olivia." *They* or *them* can be used instead of "Mom and Dad, otherwise known as my parents."

Let's start with three words you use to talk about yourself: *I*, *me*, *my*. Here they are in action.

> *I ordered the salami and cheese sub with pickles.*
> *Give **me** the salami and cheese sub with pickles.*
> *This is **my** salami and cheese sub with pickles.*

Notice how you can use stand-ins to talk about a person without using that person's name. In this case, you're using *I*, *me*, and *my* to talk about yourself. There are similar sets of words for referring to other people without naming them. Say you want to talk about your older brother, Wilbur. You can put him in the same picture, without using his name.

> ***He*** *ordered the booger and onion wrap.* (He's not your favorite sibling.)

*Give **him** the booger and onion wrap.*

*This is **his** booger and onion wrap.*

Now do the same thing with your three-year-old sister, Olivia.

***She** ordered the hot dog with ketchup.*

*Give **her** the hot dog with ketchup.*

*This is **her** hot dog with ketchup.*

You can even do it with multiple people, like Mom and Dad, otherwise known as your parents.

***They** ordered the anchovy and pineapple pizza.*

*Give **them** the anchovy and pineapple pizza.*

*This is **their** anchovy and pineapple pizza.*

See how neatly that works?

Stand-ins are a wonderful invention, and amazingly useful. The main problem with them is which one to pick when you have a choice: *I* or *me*? *She* or *her*? *He* or *him*? *They* or *them*? This is where teeny-weeny words can cause big headaches.

HIDE-AND-SEEK

It's decision time, but don't choke up. Nobody's keeping score except you. Which of these two sentences is right?

♦ *Derek and **I** never miss batting practice.*

♦ *Derek and **me** never miss batting practice.*

Which would you choose, *I* or *me*? To find the answer, let's play hide-and-seek. First of all, hide Derek, since he's not the guy we're worried about. Next, seek the right stand-in.

. . . *[I* or *me] never miss batting practice.*

Which sounds right? (Hint: Say them aloud, one at a time.)

. . . *I never miss batting practice.*

. . . *me never miss batting practice.*

What does your ear tell you? Would you ever in a million years say, "*Me* never miss batting practice"? Of course not. The answer you seek is *I.* OK, now let's put Derek back.

Derek and I never miss batting practice.

Wasn't that easy? Here's why this system works.

A stand-in (like *I* or *me*) can be confusing when it's paired with something else (like *Derek*). But the stand-in has to make sense all by itself. So the thing to do is hide *Derek*, then seek the stand-in. Consider each one (*I* or *me*) by itself. You'll choose the right stand-in every time.

Now try an all-new puzzle.

♦ *Count Olaf is mean to you and I.*
♦ *Count Olaf is mean to you and me.*

Which is right: *you and I* or *you and me*? First hide *you*, since it doesn't change. This simplifies things considerably, leaving us with

 *Count Olaf is mean to . . . [**I** or **me**].*

Now seek the stand-in. Consider one at a time.

 *Count Olaf is mean to . . . **I**.*

 *Count Olaf is mean to . . . **me**.*

Which one sounds better? Pretty obvious, isn't it? Here's the answer to the puzzle.

 *Count Olaf is mean to you and **me**.*

If you're in a hurry, or if you're too busy for hide-and-seek, you might be tempted to answer *Count Olaf is mean to **you and I**.* Some grammarphobes always put *I* instead of *me* at the end of a sentence. Why do they do this?

The confusion probably starts when kids first learn to talk. They're told to say, "*I* want a cookie," not "*Me* want a cookie." So they start thinking that *I* is always right, or that it's more polite. In fact, *me* is more likely to be correct at the end of a sentence.

Since you've got *I* and *me* all straightened out, let's move on to some other stand-ins. Which of these sentences would you choose?

♦ *You and **she** can play soccer with Mia.*
♦ *You and **her** can play soccer with Mia.*

Is it *you and **her**?* Or *you and **she**?* First play hide-and-seek. Hide *you*, since it stays the same. That leaves us with the real problem.

*. . . [**she** or **her**] can play soccer with Mia.*

Now seek the answer. Consider the possibilities one at a time.

*. . . **she** can play soccer with Mia.*

*. . . **her** can play soccer with Mia.*

What does your ear tell you? Right again—it's *she*! So the correct sentence is

*You and **she** can play soccer with Mia.*

Here's the same problem, at the other end of a sentence. Which one is right?

♦ *Rodney fell off his board and landed on you and **he**.*
♦ *Rodney fell off his board and landed on you and **him**.*

Is it *you and **he***? Or *you and **him***? Remember the hide-and-seek technique! Hide *you*, which doesn't change. Here are the choices.

*Rodney fell off his board and landed on . . . **he**.*

*Rodney fell off his board and landed on . . . **him**.*

I'll bet you know the answer. Your ear probably led you to *him*. So the correct sentence, all put back together, looks like this.

*Rodney fell off his board and landed on you and **him**.*

The hide-and-seek technique works with other stand-ins, too: *she* and *her*, *they* and *them*, *we* and *us*. Simply hide the word that isn't causing trouble, then seek the right stand-in. Remember, what looks like a big problem is usually only a bunch of little ones.

Bone Appétit!

As Mom and *I* walked homewardly,
A puppy followed *her* and *me.*
Both *she* and *I* were quick to see
He had adopted Mom and *me.*

At home *we* showed *him* where to pee
And where the doggy bed would be.
Then Mom and *I* made lunch for three,
A feast for *him* and Mom and *me.*

ME, MYSELF, AND I

In the contest between *I* and *me,* the booby prize often goes to *myself.* That's because people who can't decide between *I* and *me* often choose *myself* instead. They say things like, *Keira and **myself** ate in the lunchroom.* Or, *Orlando sat with Keira and **myself.*** You've probably done it yourself!

Well, I'm sorry, but that's cheating.

Don't use *myself* instead of *I* or *me.* Why? Because the *self* words are for special occasions. These words (*myself, yourself, herself, himself, themselves,* and others) aren't supposed to take the place of the regular stand-ins (*I, me, you, she, her, he, him, they, them,* and so on). They're used for two purposes, and two purposes only.

- To emphasize something. *I made the burrito all by* **myself**.
- To refer to someone already mentioned. *I looked at* **myself** *in the mirror.*

Now let's go back to the cafeteria and take another look at those sentences: *Keira and* **myself** *ate in the lunchroom. Orlando sat with Keira and* **myself**.

Do those look like either of the special occasions when it's OK to use *myself*? No, not by a long shot. Let's fix those sentences: *Keira and* **I** *ate in the lunchroom. Orlando sat with Keira and* **me**.

The next time you start to use *myself*, think again. If you're not emphasizing something, or referring to someone already mentioned in the sentence, you don't need a *self* word. Use *I* or *me* instead. Don't be *self*-ish!

MORE THAN MEETS THE *I*

Take a guess. Which of these sentences would you say is right?

♦ *Sarah is taller than* **me**.
♦ *Sarah is taller than* **I**.

This is a tough one. Some of the smartest people I know hesitate at the word *than*. What goes next, *I* or *me*? Both *I* and *me* sound good, don't they? But only

11

one is correct here. I won't keep you waiting. The answer is

Sarah is taller than I.

Why? Because what you really mean is *Sarah is taller than I am*. The answer is plain!

When you have a choice between *than I* or *than me*, there's usually something invisible lurking in the background. In the previous example, *Sarah is taller than I*, the invisible part is the word *am*. It doesn't have to be in the sentence, but you can't ignore it.

Here's a trick to help you choose between *than I* or *than me*. In your mind, restore the invisible part and then pick the words that sound right with it.

This works even with more complicated sentences. Take a look at these two.

♦ *Garfield likes chocolate-chip cookie dough more than I.*
♦ *Garfield likes chocolate-chip cookie dough more than me.*

Which do you think is correct: *more than I* or *more than me*? (Don't hyperventilate—you can't go wrong!)

In a situation like this, either one—*than I* or *than me*—could be correct, depending on what you mean. It all becomes clear when you mentally restore the invisible parts.

You might mean *Garfield likes chocolate-chip cookie dough more than I <u>do</u>.* In that case the correct sentence (with *do* hidden again) is this one.

> *Garfield likes chocolate-chip cookie dough more than I.*

Or you might mean *Garfield likes chocolate-chip cookie dough more than <u>he likes</u> me.* In that case the correct sentence (with *he likes* hidden again) goes this way.

> *Garfield likes chocolate-chip cookie dough more than me.*

Two different meanings, depending on what's invisible—and on how good a friend Garfield is!

THEY AND COMPANY:
They're, Their, Theirs
(and There and There's)

These words remind me of a roomful of Weasleys in a Harry Potter book. There seem to be half a dozen too many, all stepping on one another's feet. But if you take them one at a time, they're pretty harmless.

- *They're* is shorthand for "they are": ***They're** scared of spiders.*
- *Their* and *theirs* are the possessive forms for *they* (possessives are words that show ownership or belonging): ***Their** phobias are **theirs** alone.*

- *There* is a place word (like *here*), and *there's* is shorthand for "there is": **There's** *a spider over* **there**.

A poem might help sort things out.

The Dinner Guests

They seem to have taken on airs.
They're ever so rude with *their* stares.
They get *there* quite late,
There's a hand in your plate,
And *they're* eating what's not even *theirs*.

CHAPTER 2

PLURALS BEFORE SWINE
Sometimes There's More Than One

With grammar, it's always something. If it's not one thing, it's two (or four, or eight), and that's where plurals come in.

Plural means more than one. Without plural words, we'd have to talk about one thing at a time. You couldn't eat a bag of *peanuts*, you'd have to eat *peanut* after *peanut* after *peanut*. But language is very handy. A *bagful* here and a *bagful* there and—hey!—you've got *bagfuls*. See? There's nothing we can't have more of, even *tarantulas*, because anything that can be singular can also be plural.

See if you can find the eleven plurals in this poem. (Hint: There's one in the title.)

You've Got Plurals!

When you've got ants in your pants,
Or cheeses from France,
Or grouches on couches,
Or scratches and ouches,
Or pigs wearing pearls,
Why, then you've got plurals!

If you know how to talk, you know how to make a single (or singular) thing plural. Most of the time, you add a hissing or buzzing sound at the end. That's how *cat* becomes *cats*, how *match* becomes *matches*, and how *puppy* becomes *puppies*.

The sound you add can be spelled *s* or *es* or *ies*, depending on the word you start with. In general, plurals are a piece (or should I say pieces?) of cake.

Of course, some plural words don't fit the mold. That's one of the things that make them interesting. You already know that *children* (not "childs") shouldn't play with *knives* (not "knifes"). And *geese* (not "gooses") share the barn with *mice* (not "mouses"). You may have picked up some other unusual plurals, like *phenomena* and *bacteria* (although you should do your best NOT to pick up bacteria!).

Sometimes a word is all-purpose and can be either singular or plural. The animal kingdom is full of words that can mean either one critter or many, like *fish, deer, moose, vermin, elk, sheep,* and *swine.*

But first things first. Here are the three most important rules you need for making things multiply.

THE s RULE

- To make most things (including names) plural, add *s* to the end.

> *Worms, germs, pickles, harmonicas.*
> *Earls, squirrels, nickels, Veronicas.*
> *Tickets, crickets, buckets,* and *bubbles.*
> *Bumpkins, pumpkins, Flintstones,* and *Rubbles.*

THE es RULE

- If the thing (it might be a name) ends in *s, sh, ch, x,* or *z,* add *es* to the end.

> *Foxes, boxes, scratches,* and *itches.*
> *Faxes, Maxes, waltzes,* and *britches.*
> *Joshes, galoshes, wretches,* and *highnesses.*
> *Dresses, Tesses, pluses,* and *minuses.*

THE ies RULE

- If a thing ends in *y,* drop the *y* and add *ies.*

Tummies, bellies, panties, and *fannies.*
Duties, beauties, aunties, and *grannies.*
Fries, flies, spies, and *monstrosities.*
Mummies, sorceries, and *curiosities.*

HOWEVER . . .

Here comes a "however" (which, as you all know, is a big "but"). There are two exceptions to the *ies* rule for *y* words.

- Add just *s* to a name that ends in *y* (like *Jenny* or *Tommy*).
- Add just *s* to a word (like *boy* or *key*) if the *y* comes after *a, e, i, o,* or *u.* (In case you're wondering, these letters are called vowels.)

Here are the two exceptions at work.

Monkeys, donkeys, Sallys, and *Sidneys.*
Saturdays, holidays, alleys, and *kidneys.*
Turkeys on *gurneys, cowboys* on *journeys.*
Subways and *X-rays* and *guys* with *attorneys.*

There you have it: plurals in a nutshell (or several nutshells). Those rules are all you need to make most words into plurals.

I say "most," because sometimes a special word calls for special treatment. You might wonder how to make a last name like *Sanchez* or *Peepers* plural. Or you might wonder how to refer to more than one *spoonful,* or *brother-in-law,* or *nutshell.*

And what about words ending in *o*? Some of them

are special cases, too. Since those are simple, we'll look at them first.

ONE POTATO, TWO POTATO?

Most words that end in *o* are easy to make plural. Just add *s*. *His favorite **tattoos** are **hippos** and **rhinos**.*

But a handful of *o* words, including one of the first you learned (the word *no*), insist on being different. You make them plural by adding *es*. If you're not sure, check the dictionary. This poem includes some of the more common exceptions.

> Finicky *heroes*
> Prefer *torpedoes*
> To fried green *tomatoes*
> And lumpy mashed *potatoes*.

KEEPING UP WITH THE *JONESES*

You already know how to make names plural: add either *s* or *es*. This is true for both first and last names. In most cases, you add just *s*, even if the name ends in *y*. But you add *es* if the name ends in a hiss, a shush, or a buzz (*s*, *sh*, *ch*, *x*, or *z*).

*The Greek goddess **Artemis** and the master criminal **Artemis** are just a couple of **Artemises**.*

> *Our team has three **Rodriguezes** and two*
> ***Williamses**.*
> *There are seventy-two **Joneses** in the phone book,*
> *including two **Marys**, three **Henrys**, and four*
> ***Jerrys**.*
> *The **DiCaprios** and the **Morleskieviches** had*
> *dinner with the **Simpsons** and the **Bagginses** at*
> *the home of the **Osbournes**.*

BUILDING BLOCKS

Some words are like small construction projects. We call them compound words because they're compounded (or made up) of two or more smaller words. For instance, you get *toolbox* by combining *tool* and *box*, and you get *brother-in-law* by adding *brother* plus *in* plus *law*. As you can see, sometimes the parts are squished together and sometimes they're connected by little lines.

So how do you make a plural out of a combination word? If the combo is squished together, it's easy. Just add the usual plural ending to the end.

> *The **schoolchildren** left **fingerprints** on the*
> ***motorcycles**.*
> *The **taxicabs** were stuffed with **toolboxes**,*
> ***bookcases**, and **footstools**.*

Things get a bit complicated when the parts are connected by those little lines (they're called hyphens). Where do you put the plural ending? Is it *brothers-in-law* or *brother-in-laws*? Here's the story. Find the most important part of the combo, the part that would make sense if it were there all by itself. This part gets the plural ending.

> *Those **commanders**-in-chief are **mothers**-to-be.*
>
> *The Duke's **sisters**-in-law are **ladies**-in-waiting.*

If you can't decide which part is most important, remember that you have a friend with the answers. Yes, the dictionary. Look it up!

IFS, ANDS, OR BUTS

When you're on your best behavior (and that's your normal behavior, right?), it's a good idea to squeeze in a few pleases and thank-yous. See, even *please* and *thank-you* can be plural.

There are times when we need to make plurals out of routine words like *yes, no, maybe,* and *please.* No problem. Just follow the rules you already know for making words plural. *Jimmy asked Mom five times to borrow her toaster and got three **noes** and two **maybes**, but no **yeses**.* Whoops, here comes another poem.

Whys Up

Ups and *downs* and *ins* and *outs,*
Forevers and *nevers* and *whys.*
Befores and *afters, dos* and *don'ts,*
Farewells and *hellos* and *good-byes.*

Life is a string of *perhapses,*
A medley of *whens* and *so whats.*
We rise on our *yeses* and *maybes,*
Then fall on our *noes* and our *buts.*

PLURALS OF WISDOM

Sometimes you need to make a plural out of a letter all by itself. Let's say you want to ask someone how many times the letter *a* appears in "Alabama," or the letter *i* in "Mississippi." If you added just an *s* to the letter to make it plural, the result would be hard to read. *How many **as** are in Alabama, and how many **is** are in Mississippi?* See what I mean?

Many experts recommend adding a little mark right after the letter to make the plural easier to see. *How many **a's** are in Alabama, and how many **i's** are in Mississippi?* I think this is a wise idea, but do it only for single letters. *Those who mind their **p's** and **q's** get **A's** for good behavior.*

By the way, those little marks are called apostrophes. You'll learn about them (and other punctuation marks) later. For more, see pages 118-19.

FINGER FOOD: *This* and *That*

We all know that it's not polite to point—not with our fingers, at any rate. Fortunately, we don't have to use our fingers. We can use words to do the pointing.

We use *this* to point to one thing and *that* to point to another. We use *these* and *those* to point to more than one thing at a time. Didn't I tell you? There are plurals for everything.

You can use pointing words all by themselves: ***This*** *is awesome.* ***That*** *is outrageous. I'll take* ***these***. *You take* ***those***.

Or if you want to be more specific, you can use them along with the things they point to. ***This burrito*** *is awesome.* ***That salsa*** *is outrageous. I'll take* ***these chips***. *You take* ***those beans***.

THE WHOLE ENCHILADA: *Kinds, Sorts, Types*

Now let's add some ingredients to our burrito. No, I'm not talking about cheese or sauce or refried beans. I mean words like *kind*, *sort*, *type*, and *style* (along with their plurals: *kinds*, *sorts*, *types*, and *styles*).

You've probably heard sentences like this one: "I hate these kind of burritos." If it sounds wrong to you, you're right. It should be ***this kind*** *of* ***burrito*** or ***these kinds*** *of* ***burritos***.

Certain words, like certain foods, go together naturally. Refried beans are great with cheese, but not with grape jelly. Similarly, a singular word (like *kind*) goes with a singular word (like *burrito*), and a plural (like *kinds*) goes with a plural (like *burritos*). Why? For the same reason that one tortilla makes one burrito, and two tortillas make two.

Here are some examples of ingredients that go well together.

> *"I enjoy **this kind** of **taco**," said Margo.*
>
> *"**These kinds** of **tacos** are boring," said Phoebe.*
>
> *"I prefer **that sort** of **salsa**," said Margo.*
>
> *"**Those sorts** of **salsas** give me heartburn," said Phoebe.*
>
> *"**That type** of **nacho** is my favorite," said Margo.*
>
> *"Jerks eat **those types** of **nachos**," said Phoebe.*
>
> *"**This style** of **enchilada** makes me pig out," said Margo.*
>
> *"**These styles** of **enchiladas** make me puke," said Phoebe.*

FUN WITH *FUNGUSES*

There's something weird about *fungus*. In case you haven't noticed, it has two ways of being plural: *funguses* and *fungi*. (As words go, it's full of fun.)

Cactus also has two plurals: *cactuses* and *cacti*. How prickly is that!

So what's going on? I'm glad you asked.

Words from Latin and other foreign languages sometimes keep their old flavor long after they've been absorbed into English. They can still become plural the old way (*fungi* and *cacti*). But they've also adopted new, English-style endings (as in *funguses* and *cactuses*). So one person may say *fungi* and another *funguses*; one may say *cacti* and another *cactuses*. They're all correct.

As the years go by, these foreign-born words tend to lose their old plural endings. Here's a list of English-style plurals that are now more common than the older versions: *appendixes, beaus, chateaus, formulas, gymnasiums, indexes, memorandums, octopuses, referendums, stadiums, syllabuses, symposiums, tableaus, ultimatums,* and *virtuosos.*

Some foreign words are more stubborn, though. These preferred plurals have kept their foreign endings: *algae, analyses, bacteria, crises, criteria, hypo-*

theses, *oases*, *parentheses*, *phenomena*, and *vertebrae*. But check back in fifty years. By then, fossil hunters may be digging up dinosaur *vertebras* instead of *vertebrae*.

Incidentally, if you're a bug collector (excuse me, a junior entomologist), you may wonder about the plural of *antenna*. Good question. An insect's feelers are *antennae*. But the gizmos that pick up radio signals are *antennas*.

Didn't I say that plurals were interesting? Just imagine a world without plurals, a world with only one of everything. Not only is this biologically impossible, but try getting a soccer team together! And parties are out of the question. No, you simply can't have a world without plurals. Just ask Noah.

What Noah Knew

The ark was filled symmetrically:
A boy for every girl.
It owed its singularity
To plural after plural.

YOURS TRULY
Possessives and the Possessed

When something belongs to you, it is yours. Does this make you selfish? Not necessarily. In fact, you can't help having some things—like your whiny brother or your icky sister or your allergies or your claustrophobia.

The point is that the world is full of things that belong to us or to other people. Some of them are material things (a toe, a toothbrush, or a toad, for instance), while others aren't (an idea, a problem, or a nightmare). I'll bet you don't feel very possessive about your nightmares and would be quite happy to give them away!

There are many ways to talk about things you possess. You can say, "This toad belongs to me." Or, "I am the lawful owner of this toad." But it's often

handier to use a possessive word, like *my* and *mine*,
your and *yours*, *our* and *ours*, and so on. You might say,
"This is *my* toad." Or, "This toad is *mine*."

Now let's put the toad down and watch some possessive words in action.

IS THAT *YOUR* WARTHOG?

You're already familiar with a lot of possessive words. You've been using them for years. In case you need a reminder, here's how they work.

*This hound dog is **mine**. It is **my** hound dog.*
*This groundhog is **yours**. It is **your** groundhog.*
*This warthog is **hers**. It is **her** warthog.*
*This polliwog is **his**. It is **his** polliwog.*
*This hedgehog is **theirs**. It is **their** hedgehog.*
*This bulldog is **ours**. It is **our** bulldog.*

That was easy. But what about words like *Timmy*, *godmother*, and *blog*? Yes, they can possess things, too. ***Timmy's** fairy godmother has a blog. The **blog's** photo gallery shows the fairy **godmother's** wand.*

You can make a possessive out of any word that stands for a person, place, or thing (remember, we call these words nouns). Here's how.

HAPPY ENDINGS

All you need to make almost any word possessive is an apostrophe (') and the letter *s*. Sometimes you use both of them together (*'s*), and sometimes you use the apostrophe alone ('). It all depends on how the word ends and whether it is singular or plural (that is, one thing or more than one).

- If the word is singular, always add *'s*, even if it already ends with an *s*. ***Klaus's*** *family escaped when Count **Olaf's** back was turned.*
- If the word is plural and doesn't already end with *s*, add *'s*. *Violet studied the **children's** menu while Klaus was in the **men's** room.*
- If the word is plural and ends in *s*, add just the apostrophe ('). *The **waiters'** strike ruined the **Baudelaires'** meal.*

Some people get hyper when they have to make a name (like *Murphy*) or another word (like *witch*) both plural and possessive. If you're one of those people, relax. Here's the deal. First make the singular word into a plural (***Murphys*** or ***witches***). Then add an apostrophe at the end to make the word possessive (*the **Murphys'** vacation* or ***witches'** brooms*). Remember, the apostrophe goes right after the plural ending.

And don't be fooled by a name or other word that ends in *s*. Take *Willis*, for example—or rather, a couple of people named *Willis*. Let's say they own something together, perhaps a van. First add *es* to

Willis to make the name plural (**Willises**). Then simply add an apostrophe to the end to make the name possessive (*the* **Willises'** *van*).

The same goes for all words that end in a hissing, shushing, or buzzing sound (*s, sh, ch, x,* or *z*). You add *es* to make them plural, and then tack on an apostrophe to make them possessive. *The* **Tishes'** *oak tree dropped acorns into the* **Birches'** *pool, the* **Alexes'** *driveway, the* **Sanchezes'** *flower bed, and the* **Higginses'** *tennis court.*

For more on making names plural, see pages 20-21.

IT'S OR ITS?

An apostrophe does not always mean that a word is possessive. Apostrophes can also stand for letters that have been removed. Take *it's,* a squashed-together word (called a contraction) that is short for "it is." The apostrophe in *it's* stands for the missing letter *i* in *is*. Let's put *it's* to work (with a little help from Scabbers).

When **it's** *time for dinner, the rat squeaks.*

The plain and simple *its,* the one without the punctuation, is the possessive form.

Ron says **its** *feeding time is five o'clock.*

Here's an easy way to keep *it's* and *its* straight.

- If you can substitute "it is," use *it's*.

A poem may help you sort out *it's* and *its*.

It Wit

This itsy-bitsy mystery
Sure used to give me fits.
How come there's an apostrophe
In *it's* but not in *its*?

The answer to this little quiz:
The longer *it's* stands for "it is,"
While the *its* that's less impressive
Is the one that's a possessive.

WHO'S OR WHOSE?

This problem is a first cousin of the one above (*it's* versus *its*). In this case, *who's*, with the apostrophe, is shorthand for "who is." The plain and simple *whose* is the possessive form.

Whose *rat is the one* **who's** *squeaking?*

You remember how to keep *it's* and *its* straight. Here's a similar trick for getting *who's* and *whose* right.

- If you can substitute "who is," use *who's*.

YOU'RE OR YOUR?

As you've probably guessed, *you're* is shorthand for "you are." Plain old *your*, without the punctuation, is the possessive form.

> *Your rat thinks **you're** starving him.*

I'll bet you already know what comes next.

- If you can substitute "you are," use *you're.*

THEY'RE OR THEIR?

Same principle here. *They're* is short for "they are." The one without the punctuation, *their*, is the possessive form.

> *Their rats hiss when **they're** hungry.*

The rule (as if you didn't know):

- If you can substitute "they are," use *they're.*

THERE'S NO *THEIR* THERE

What's wrong with this sentence? *Someone parked their bike in Lance's spot.*

That doesn't sound so bad, does it? But the sentence has a small problem there (hint) in the middle. The problem is *their.* Here's why.

Their, like *they* and *them*, is plural. But the "someone" who parked in the wrong spot is just one person, not a *they*. The sentence mistakenly puts a plural word (*their*) where a singular word (like *his* or *her*) belongs.

This is an extremely common mistake. Why? Because many people are reluctant to use *his* or *her* when they aren't referring to anyone in particular. They may not even know whether the "someone" is a he or a she. So they compromise by using *their*. Sometimes compromise is a good thing, but not in this case.

There's a better way to refer to that special "someone." In fact, there are quite a few better ways. Try using one of these alternatives.

> *Someone parked **his** bike in Lance's spot.*
> *Someone parked **her** bike in Lance's spot.*
> *Someone parked **his or her** bike in Lance's spot.*

There are still other ways of avoiding mistakes with *their*. You can take it out, as many editors do, and avoid the problem altogether. Like this:

> *Someone parked a bike in Lance's spot.*
> *Someone's bike is parked in Lance's spot.*
> *Someone parked in Lance's spot.*
> *There's a bike parked in Lance's spot.*

Someone isn't the only singular word that people mistakenly treat like a plural. Others include *somebody, anybody, anyone, everybody, everyone, nobody,* and *no one.* Yes, all of these are singular, even *everybody* and *everyone.* I can prove it!

We don't say, "Everybody are allergic," do we? No. We say, "Everybody is allergic." And we also say, "Somebody is itchy." And, "No one is scratching." We use *is* instead of *are* with all those words. And *is*, as I'm sure you know, is singular.

So the next time you get an itch to refer to a singular word like *somebody* or *everyone* with a plural like *their*, don't do it. Try scratching instead.

ACTION FIGURES
Words That Do the Work

Some words work harder than others. They're called verbs, and they give the other words something to do. Without a verb, there's nothing going on. You have a bunch of unemployed words standing around with their hands in their pockets. Here's what I'm talking about.

Homer . . . like a walrus.

Not much point to that, is there? Think of all the things it could mean. Let's add a few action words, or verbs, and you'll see.

*Homer **waddles** like a walrus.*

*Homer **chews** like a walrus.*

*Homer **snores** like a walrus.*

I could go on, but you get the idea. There are two points to be made here. First, Homer doesn't have very refined manners. Second, a verb tells you what's happening. It lets you know what someone (or something) is doing. Without an action word, all you have is a string of words. Add one, and you've got a sentence! No wonder the verb is often the most important word in a sentence.

It's usually easy to spot an action word. Just look for where the action is. Let's give Homer a rest and try out some verbs on a more palatable subject. How many action words can you find in this poem?

Meatball Hero

My meatball fell onto the floor
And rolled across Long Island.
It bounced into a cargo ship
And sailed away to Thailand.

My meatball hopped aboard a bus,
And hitched a ride to Rome,
Then sneaked into a post office
And mailed itself back home.

If you found eight action words, you got them all. Here they are: *fell, rolled, bounced, sailed, hopped, hitched, sneaked,* and *mailed.* How's that for action?

COUCH POTATOES:
Less Obvious Actions

Some actions speak louder than others. As we know, a verb tells us what's going on. But what's happening may not be as obvious as rolling or bouncing or hopping. If you exist, for example, you're doing something, right? You're existing. And if you feel weird, you're doing something, too. You're feeling. So let's wake up the snoring Homer and give him some less obvious things to do.

> Homer **looks** like a walrus.
>
> Homer **smells** like a walrus.
>
> Homer **is** like a walrus.

Yes, those words (*looks*, *smells*, and *is*) are verbs, too.

Now, remember that well-traveled meatball? It doesn't always bounce around and hitch rides. Sometimes it just sits in a bowl of spaghetti or a sandwich and contemplates its fate. See how many verbs you can find this time.

Beef Interlude

My meatball seems preoccupied.
Its outlook is abysmal.
It has no sense of humor
And its mood appears quite dismal.

I think I know the reason
Why it looks so darned depressed.
It lost all its tomato sauce
And now it feels undressed.

If you found nine, you're a champ: *seems, is, has, appears, think, know, looks, lost,* and *feels.* If you missed one or two, no big deal. Once you get used to them, it's easy to spot the sneaky verbs.

SUBJECT MATTER: Who's Doing What

Verbs do a lot, but they can't act by themselves. An action word needs someone or something (Shrek, for example) to do the acting. That's where the subject comes in.

The subject of a sentence is who or what is doing the action. In the sentence *Shrek burps like an ogre,* the subject is *Shrek.*

Subjects are often nouns. A noun, you'll recall, is a name for something—a person (like *Shrek*), a place (like *Duloc*), or a thing (like *earwax* or *happiness* or *evil*). But subjects can also be pronouns (remember, these are words, like *he* or *they,* that stand in for nouns). And subjects can also be phrases (groups of words, like *Shrek and Fiona,* or *the talking donkey*).

Just as a subject can have more than one verb (*Shrek belches, snorts, and farts*), a verb can have more than one subject (**Shrek and Fiona** *burp*).

Here's where things become interesting. Subjects and verbs have to get along together. Singular subjects (like *Shrek*) must have singular verbs (like *burps*), and plural subjects (like *ogres,* or *Shrek and Fiona*) must have plural verbs (like *burp*). Singulars go with singulars, and plurals with plurals. That's why *Shrek* **burps**, but *ogres* **burp**. If you speak English, this is something you already know without being told. You wouldn't say, "Shrek burp," would you? Not unless you were doing an impression of a troll.

Here are some other examples of subjects and verbs playing nicely together.

> Shrek **makes** *earwax candles. Shrek and Fiona* **make** *earwax candles.*
>
> *The talking donkey* **chatters** *like a monkey. Talking donkeys* **chatter** *like monkeys.*
>
> *Happiness* **is** *a warm ogre. Warm ogres* **are** *happy.*

No surprises there. However, choosing the right verb is sometimes tricky. You'll be up to the challenge if you take your verbs one by one (which is how you encounter them, after all).

MISSING IN ACTION:
Where's the Subject?

It's not snack time yet, but consider this sentence.

Have a cookie.

Yes, it's a sentence, all right. But where's the subject?

As we all know by now, a verb can't act by itself. It needs a subject to do the acting. But sometimes the subject seems to be missing in action. What's going on? When we say, "Have a cookie," where's the subject?

The subject is there (trust me), although it's hidden. Can you tell what it is?

Yes, it's the person we're speaking to. What we're actually saying is something like this: ***You**, have a cookie.*

When we suggest or demand that someone do something, the subject is often a hidden *you*. I'm talking about sentences like these.

Save me a cupcake.

Look at the icing!

Pass the milk, please.

Go!

OK, you've been patient. Have a cookie!

WILL THE REAL SUBJECT PLEASE STAND UP?

Let's say your dog (we'll call him Fang) has had an action-packed day. In other words, he's a mess. Which sentence would you choose?

♦ *My dog Fang **is** all muddy.*
♦ *My dog Fang **are** all muddy.*

That was easy. The subject of the sentence, *Fang*, is a single dog, so he gets a singular verb: *My dog Fang **is** all muddy.*

Now let's add a few of Fang's less appealing qualities. Which sentence is right?

♦ *My nosy, wayward, and rambunctious dog Fang **is** all muddy.*
♦ *My nosy, wayward, and rambunctious dog Fang **are** all muddy.*

I'm sure you weren't fooled by Fang's multifaceted personality. He's still just one dog. A single subject stays singular, no matter how many words you use to describe it. So the correct sentence is *My nosy, wayward, and rambunctious dog Fang **is** all muddy.*

Note Words that help describe nouns (like *nosy*, *wayward*, and *rambunctious*) are called adjectives. Words that help describe verbs (like *greedily*, *sloppily*, and *ravenously*) are called adverbs. *Fang eats* **greedily**, **sloppily**, *and* **ravenously**.

Now we'll toss in a few of Fang's muddy parts. Which is right?

- *My dog Fang—his tail, his ears, his paws—***is** *all muddy.*
- *My dog Fang—his tail, his ears, his paws—***are** *all muddy.*

Any ideas? Remember, before you can pick the right verb, you have to know the subject, since the two must match. And the real subject isn't always easy to see. Sometimes a lot of messy details get in the way and muddy the water.

In this case, the subject of the sentence is still *Fang*. And even if you added a dozen more messy parts, it would still be *Fang*. Since the subject hasn't changed, the verb doesn't change. The correct sentence: *My dog Fang—his tail, his ears, his paws—***is** *all muddy.*

If you got that one, give yourself a treat. Now try another. Which sentence is right?

- *My dog Fang, like other dogs in the suburbs,* **needs** *a place to run.*
- *My dog Fang, like other dogs in the suburbs,* **need** *a place to run.*

Again the thing to do is zero in on the subject. Who or what *needs* or *need* a place to run? Yes, it's *Fang* again! And since the subject is singular, it gets a singular verb: *My dog Fang, like other dogs in the suburbs,* **needs** *a place to run.*

Don't be distracted by extra information that comes between a subject and a verb.

One last tip. Expressions like *along with, as well as, in addition to,* and *together with,* inserted between the subject and the verb, don't change the verb: *My dog Fang, along with the other dogs in the neighborhood,* **is** *all muddy.*

I think it's time to get out the garden hose and give Fang and his friends a bath.

TEA FOR TWO:
When Subjects Multiply

Plural verbs are handy to have around. If they didn't exist, we'd have to talk about one person or thing at a time. Communicating would take a lot longer. We'd be forced to say things like this:

> *Lois* **is** *in the kitchen drinking tea and Hal* **is** *in the kitchen drinking tea.*

Sounds pretty clunky, doesn't it? Thank goodness we don't have to do that. When the subject of a sentence has two parts, like *Lois* and *Hal,* we can join them with *and,* then use a plural verb.

Lois and Hal **are** *in the kitchen drinking tea.*

Pretty nifty! Two singular subjects, joined by *and,* add up to a plural subject.

Now here's a tricky question. What do you do if two singular subjects are joined by *or* instead of *and*? Which of these sentences is correct?

♦ *Either Lois or Hal* **makes** *breakfast each morning.*
♦ *Either Lois or Hal* **make** *breakfast each morning.*

Give up? Here's the rule. If the parts on each side of *or* are singular, the verb should be singular, too. So the answer is *Either Lois or Hal* **makes** *breakfast each morning.*

That makes sense, doesn't it? So what do you do when the parts on each side of *or* are plural? Choose the correct sentence.

♦ *Either pancakes or eggs* **is** *always available.*
♦ *Either pancakes or eggs* **are** *always available.*

I'll bet you got that one. Since the parts on each side of *or* are plural, the verb has to be plural, too: *Either pancakes or eggs* **are** *always available.*

So far, so good. But things are about to get sticky. What do you do when the part on one side of *or*

46

is singular and the part on the other side is plural? Should the verb, or action word, be singular or plural? See if you can decide which of these is correct.

♦ *Either pancakes or toast **is** always available.*
♦ *Either pancakes or toast **are** always available.*

Don't panic. This isn't as hard as it looks. If the part that's closer to the verb is singular, the verb is singular. If the part that's closer to the verb is plural, the verb is plural. So the right choice is *Either pancakes or toast **is** always available.*

Now let's switch around the pancakes and the toast (it's OK to play with your food here). Which of these examples is correct?

♦ *Either toast or pancakes **is** always available.*
♦ *Either toast or pancakes **are** always available.*

Remember, look for the part that's closer to the verb. In this case, the closer part is *pancakes*. And *pancakes* is plural, right? So the verb is plural, too: *Either toast or pancakes **are** always available.*

This is making me hungry.

ALL TENSED UP

As I've said, the verb is often the most important word in a sentence. That's because it does so many jobs. Besides telling us what's going on, the verb also tells us when. That's why we say, *Cameron **belched** yesterday, she **belches** today, and she **will belch** tomorrow.* (Boys aren't the only ones with embarrassing habits!)

Verbs, like people, dress up differently for different occasions. They put on different outfits, called tenses, to show when something happens, or happened, or will happen, and so on. In fact, Cameron just belched her way through the three basic tenses: present, past, and future.

As I'm sure you know, there's another way of talking about something in the present, the past, or the future. You can say that Cameron *is eating*, or *was*

eating, or *will be eating*. For now, though, let's stick to the three basic tenses.

If a sentence has only one action word, it's easy to tell when the action takes place. *Cameron **eats** too much* (present). *Cameron **ate** too much* (past). *Cameron **will eat** too much* (future).

Many sentences, though, have more than one verb. That's because there's more than one thing going on. When all the actions happen at the same time, there's no problem. We put all the verbs in the same tense.

Here's an example with all the action words in the present: *On Saturdays, Cameron **rises** at 8:15, **drinks***

juice, **showers**, and **goes** to the mall. Here's one with all the verbs in the past: *Last Saturday, she **rose** at 8:15, **drank** juice, **showered**, and **went** to the mall.*

That's easy enough. But when the different actions in a sentence happen at different times, the verbs need to dress differently, or put on different tenses.

See if you can name the tenses in these sentences:

> *Cameron **burps** now because she **ate** too much this morning.*

> *Mike **thinks** she **will eat** too much for lunch and **will burp** again.*

Yes, *burps* is in the present tense, *ate* is in the past, *thinks* is present, *will eat* is in the future tense, and *will burp* is future, too. Present, past, and future, all in the same breath—or perhaps I should say burp.

Speaking of burps, give yourself a pat on the back. You've now completed your basic training in verbs, the action figures of English. In the next chapter, you'll see some real action. Your mission, should you decide to accept it . . .

CHAPTER 5

WORKING OUT
Action Figures in Action

If you're like most kids, you use hundreds of verbs a day. Just think of all the action words that you speak, read, and write, from the time you get up in the morning till it's time to go to bed: *yawn, stretch, itch, dribble, barf, splash, pinch, squeeze, gobble, surf, bump, slouch, google, stumble, poop, jerk, slide, gargle, slurp, whoop, toss, wallop, shrink, wiggle, sizzle, boogie,* and on and on and on.

Most of the time, you don't have to think too much about how to use a verb. You do it automatically, and you get it right. But once in a while, the autopilot doesn't work. (Crash!) In these situations, you need a real pilot, not an automatic one.

In the pages to come, you'll learn how to handle action words when the action heats up and the answers aren't so obvious.

THERE'S SOMETHING FISHY

Here's a riddle for you. What's fishy about *there*?

Answer: The word *there*, like *fish*, can be either singular or plural.

With *fish*, of course, there's no mystery: one *fish* is singular and a zillion *fish* plural. But some people have a hard time deciding whether the word *there* should be used with a singular or a plural verb, especially when it comes at the beginning of a sentence. That's no surprise, since *there* seems to have a hard time making up its own mind.

Now here's another riddle. Which sentence is correct?

♦ ***There is*** *a fly in my soup!*
♦ ***There are*** *lumps in the gravy!*

Don't spend too much time on this one. Both are right.

When a sentence starts with *there,* the next word might be *is* or it might be *are*. The clue is what comes after that. If what follows is singular (like *fly*), use *there is*. If it's plural (like *lumps*), use *there are*.

Here's why. The word *there* is a phantom subject. In the first example, the real subject is *fly*. In the second, the real subject is *lumps*. If the subject is hard for you to see, just delete *there* in your mind (remember, it's only

a phantom) and mentally turn the sentence around: *A **fly is** in my soup! And **lumps are** in the gravy!*

Even when people know the difference between *there is* and *there are*, they often mess up when they use *there's*. They seem to think it's good for all occasions. Not so. The word *there's* is short for "there is." It's not a substitute for "there are."

Now, which of these is correct?

♦ ***There's*** *a fly in my soup!*
♦ ***There's*** *lumps in the gravy!*

The first is right, of course. What should the second one be? ***There are*** *lumps in the gravy!*

I think there's time here for a corny joke.

Man in restaurant: "Waiter, what is this fly doing in my soup?"
Waiter: "The backstroke."

ALL ABOARD!

All, any, and *none* are two-faced words. Sometimes they're singular and sometimes they're plural. So how do you tell them apart? Should you say, ***All is*** *aboard the Hogwarts Express*? Or, ***All are*** *aboard the Hogwarts Express*?

Fortunately, there's a foolproof way to use *all, any,* and *none* correctly. Ask yourself whether you're talking about a single thing (*magic, potion, poison*), or more than one thing (*wands, wizards, spells*).

If you mean a single thing, choose a singular verb, or action word. ***All*** *the magic* ***is*** *gone.* ***Is any*** *potion left?* ***None*** *of the poison* ***is*** *working.* The same is true, even if the *magic,* the *potion,* and the *poison* disappear. ***All is*** *gone.* ***Is any*** *left?* ***None is*** *working.*

If you mean more than one thing, choose a plural verb: ***All*** *the wands* ***are*** *broken.* ***Are any*** *wizards on the premises?* ***None*** *of the spells* ***are*** *working.* The principle is the same, even if the *wands, wizards,* and *spells* vanish. ***All are*** *broken.* ***Are any*** *on the premises?* ***None are*** *working.*

OK, back to our original question. Should you say, ***All is*** *aboard the Hogwarts Express?* Or, ***All are*** *aboard the Hogwarts Express?*

Either one is right, depending on what you mean. *All* is singular if you're talking about a singular thing, like *luggage.* But *all* is plural if you're talking about a plural thing, like *students.* ***All*** *the first-year students* ***are*** *aboard, and* ***all*** *their luggage* ***is*** *aboard.*

One more thing. Many grown-ups mistakenly believe that *none* always means "not one" and is always singular. Not true! In fact, *none* is plural most of the time.

WISHFUL THINKING:
Was or Were?

Unless you're a very unusual kid, you probably look at yourself in the mirror and say stuff like *I wish I were taller*, or *I wish my nose were cuter*, or *I wish my hair were purple*. Everybody does.

I'm sure you're fine the way you are. But that's not the point. The point is, why do you use the word *were* when you're in this wishful mood? Why don't you say, *I wish I was taller*, or *I wish my nose was cuter*, or *I wish my hair was purple*?

In English, we have a special way of speaking wishfully. We use this wishful language to talk about things we wish were true but really aren't. We say, *I wish I were a zillionaire*, not *I wish I was a zillionaire*.

In other words, grammar has moods, just as people do. And when we're in this wishful mood, *was* becomes *were*.

You might say it's another way of daydreaming.

Wish List

I wish I *were* a hippo, wallowing in mud.
I wish I *were* a hummingbird, sipping at a bud.
I wish today *were* Saturday and I *were* not in class,
Chewing on my pencil with another test to pass.

Iffy Situations

Have you ever wondered why strange things can happen to sentences that start with *if*? For instance, the father in *Fiddler on the Roof* sings, "If I *were* a rich man," not "If I *was* a rich man." What's going on here?

As it turns out, there's a special, "iffy" kind of grammar that we use for *if* sentences when the *if* part is untrue. We say, *If I were Godzilla, I'd run amok*. We don't say, *If I was Godzilla, I'd run amok*. When we're in this iffy mood, *was* becomes *were*. (I'm assuming, of course, that you're not Godzilla!) Here are some more examples.

If I were king, nobody would flunk.

(I'm not king.)

If she were older, she'd know better.

(She's not older.)

We could go shopping if it were Saturday.

(It's not Saturday.)

But remember that not all *if* statements are false. When an *if* statement is true or may possibly be true, use *was*.

If I was rude, I apologize.

(I may have been rude.)

> *If she **was** there, I missed her.*
> (She may have been there.)
> *If yesterday **was** Thursday, I had gym class.*
> (Yesterday was Thursday.)

WILL POWER: *Will* or *Would?*

Do you flip-flop when faced with the choice of *will* or *would*?

One day, you flip: *Emeril said he **will** make Creole flapjacks for breakfast.*

On another day, you flop: *Emeril said he **would** make Creole flapjacks for breakfast.*

Which sentence is right, the flip (the one with *will*) or the flop (the one with *would*)? Both may look good, especially if you flip over flapjacks! But the correct answer is the flop: *Emeril said he **would** make Creole flapjacks for breakfast.*

So how do you choose between *will* and *would* in a sentence like that, where more than one action is going on? The clue is in the first verb, or action word, that you come to. If it's in the past tense (like *said*), use *would.* If it's in the present tense (like *says*), use *will.*

Now choose the correct sentence (no waffling, please):

♦ *Emeril* **says** *he* **will** *make Cajun waffles tomorrow.*
♦ *Emeril* **says** *he* **would** *make Cajun waffles tomorrow.*

Yes, the first one is right. Now, do you want sausages or bacon with that?

Iffy Situations: Part 2

Think of *if* as a tiny set of scales, like one you might see in a statue at a courthouse. When a sentence has *if* in it, the two sides have to be in balance. Here's what to remember.

- When the *if* side is in the present tense, you need *will* on the other side:

    If Bart **flunks** *the test, he* **will lose** *his allowance.*

- When the *if* side is in the past tense, you need *would* on the other:

    If Bart **flunked** *the test, he* **would lose** *his allowance.*

    Hey, Bart had better start studying.

PESKY LOOK-ALIKES

When you plop down into a chair, do you *sit* or do you *set*? When you stretch out flat on the floor, do you *lie* or do you *lay*? When you get up, do you *rise* or do you *raise*? (The answers: You *sit*, you *lie*, you *rise*.)

Where words are concerned, little does not mean easy. Some short words (like *sit* and *set*, *lie* and *lay*, *rise* and *raise*) can be quite confusing because they look so much alike. Once you get to know them, though, these pesky look-alikes aren't that hard to tell apart. Here's the story.

- *Lay* means "place" or "put down," and it's always followed by something (the thing being placed). The past tense of *lay* is *laid.*

   *Josh and Drake **lay** their laptops on their knees when they watch TV.*

   *Yesterday they **laid** them there.*

- *Lie*, often confused with *lay*, means "recline." The past tense of *lie* is *lay.*

   *Megan **lies** awake at night thinking up pranks.*

   *Last night she **lay** awake.*

You've probably noticed that the present tense of *lay* looks the same as the past tense of *lie*. This has tied people in knots for hundreds of years, so don't feel bad if you mess up once in a while. I sometimes get it wrong myself. I cannot lie!

That kind of *lie*, by the way, is a different word entirely, and means "tell a fib."

> *Drake **lies** to impress girls.*
> *Yesterday he **lied**.*

- *Sit* means "take a seat." (No, you don't steal it—you rest your butt on it!) The past of *sit* is *sat*.

  > *Florida **sits** in the canoe.*
  > *She **sat** there yesterday.*

- *Set* means "put" or "arrange," and it's always followed by something (the thing being placed). The past is the same as the present—*set*.

  > *Dallas **sets** the binoculars on a stump.*
  > *He **set** them there yesterday.*

- *Rise* means "go up" or "get up." The past is *rose*.

  > *Molly **rises** early for school on the reservation.*
  > *She **rose** early yesterday.*

- *Raise* means "lift" or "bring up," and it's always followed by something (the thing being lifted). The past is *raised*.

  > *Molly **raises** her hand often in class.*
  > *She **raised** it three times yesterday.*

MAYHEM
Can or May?

No, *can* and *may* do not mean the same thing, and it's important to know the difference. If your teacher says you *can* do something, that means you're capable of doing it. If he says you *may* do something, that means you're allowed to.

You *can* do a lot of things that you *may* not. For example, you *can* stand up on your desk and impersonate a monkey. (Yes, it's physically possible.) That doesn't mean you *may*.

Let me illustrate with an imaginary dialogue.

Jimmy: *"Hey, Mom, **can** I take your iPod apart?"*

Mrs. Neutron (a stickler for good English): *"Of course you **can**. But you certainly **may** not!"*

GETTING THE HANG OF *HUNG*

Pick one:

♦ *Pablo **hanged** the picture.*
♦ *Pablo **hung** the picture.*

I won't keep you hanging. The answer is *hung*. In fact, *hung* is almost always right.

Why? Well, there's no real logic to it. You simply have to memorize this one. A picture, a coat, a holiday wreath, a chandelier—almost anything you can hang up is *hung*, not *hanged*. Even after a day at the mall with friends, you have *hung out* or *hung* with them.

The other word, *hanged*, is used for only one thing: death by hanging. *The serial killer was **hanged**.*

If you can't remember that, you're suspended! (Just a little gallows humor.)

As long as we're making jokes about inappropriate things, here's another one.

What do you call someone who crushes his cornflakes? *A cereal killer.*

IT'S OK TO BE DIFFERENT

Some action words insist on being different. They don't form the past tense the usual way, by adding *ed* at the end. They prefer ending with a *t*. Most of these words come from German (remember, English is a crazy quilt of languages) and haven't quite let go of their old foreign endings.

These old-fashioned past tenses include *bent, crept, dealt, felt, kept, left, lost, meant, slept, spent, swept,* and *wept.*

Some other verbs have one foot in the old world and one in the new. As a result, they have two past tenses. The most common of these twosomes are *burned* and *burnt, dreamed* and *dreamt, dwelled* and *dwelt, kneeled* and *knelt, leaped* and *leapt.* Which one is right? The choice is up to you.

WHO NEEDS *THAT?*

There are two kinds of kids in the world: those who prefer their Froot Loops or Lucky Charms with milk, and those who like their cereal dry.

There are two kinds of writers as well. One kind sticks in *that* wherever there's room. The other avoids it like mashed turnips.

Which side is right? Neither. Here's the deal with *that.* Sometimes it makes a difference, and sometimes it doesn't.

Which of these sentences would you say is right?

♦ *Mario's mom thinks sky-diving is dangerous.*
♦ *Mario's mom thinks **that** sky-diving is dangerous.*

You can't go wrong here, because there's no wrong answer. Both sentences are correct. Some people prefer a *that.* Some don't. In this case, it's optional, which means that it's up to you.

Sometimes, however, it isn't optional. You need a *that* when, for instance, you have two action words and it's not clear when the actions happen. Let's see how a well-placed *that* can magically clear up a puzzling sentence.

Mario said on Friday his leg was broken.

Why is that sentence confusing? Because it could mean one of two things:

64

♦ *Mario said on Friday **that** his leg was broken.*
♦ *Mario said **that** on Friday his leg was broken.*

See the difference? In the first example, Mario said it on Friday. In the second, he broke his leg on Friday. That's what I mean by magic. Add a timely *that* and—presto!—problem solved.

If you're not sure whether to use *that*, ask yourself whether it would change the meaning. If so, add *that*, and be sure to put it in the right place. When *that* doesn't change the meaning, it's optional.

In these two sentences, *that* is necessary in one and optional in the other. Can you tell which is which?

♦ *Mario hopes he gets a cast.*
♦ *The doctor said on Monday Mario would be back in school.*

As you probably figured out, adding *that* wouldn't change the meaning of the first sentence, so it's optional there. Just pick whichever sentence sounds better to you: *Mario hopes he gets a cast.* Or, *Mario hopes **that** he gets a cast.*

The second example, though, isn't clear. It needs a *that* to show whether the doctor spoke on Monday, or whether Mario will be back on Monday.

♦ *The doctor said on Monday **that** Mario would be back in school.* (The doctor said it on Monday.)

♦ *The doctor said **that** on Monday Mario would be back in school.* (Mario will be back on Monday.)

• • •

So that's the story, morning glory. Now you know. Verbs are indispensable. They're also unavoidable. You can't get away from them. Of course, you can try. (Whoops—*try* is a verb!) You can run and hide. (Uh-oh, *run* and *hide* are verbs, too!) What did I tell you? Verbs are everywhere!

You Can't Avoid a Verb

You can dissolve, combust, or turn to dust,
But you can't avoid a verb.
You can readjust until you bust,
But you can't avoid a verb.

You can pout and whine. You can put up a sign:
"I'm busy! Do not disturb!"
You can mail yourself to Liechtenstein,
But you can't avoid a verb.

You can leave the state and impersonate
A Russian, a Finn, or a Serb.
You can wave a wand and evaporate,
But you can't avoid a verb.

You can hide amid a school of squid.
You can pack up and move to a burb,
Call FedEx and ship yourself off to Madrid,
But you can't avoid a verb.

SMALL MIRACLES
Incredible Shrinking Words

When something contracts, it shrinks, and a contraction is a preshrunk word. It's two words combined into one. For example, the words *do* and *not* are mushed together to make *don't*. And the words *I* and *am* are squished into *I'm*. A contraction is one of those handy things—like Velcro or cell phones—that we use all the time.

Some people, you'll find, look down their noses at a contraction. They consider it unacceptable in polite society. Not so! There's nothing wrong with combining two words into one, as long as you do it correctly. Contractions may be more informal than the stretched-out versions, but the legitimate ones are perfectly good English.

A contraction, like *I've* or *haven't*, is easy to spot because it always has a little squiggle (an apostrophe, remember?) floating in there somewhere. The apostrophe shows that some letters were lost when the two words were squeezed into one.

One of the squashed-together words is always a verb (an action word, like *have* or *is*). The other is usually the one doing the acting (*I* or *Ramona*, for example) or the word *not*, shortened to *n't*. When you join *I* and *have*, you get *I've*. When you combine *have* and *not*, you get *haven't*. And when you combine *Ramona* and *is*, you get *Ramona's*, as in *Ramona's on her way.* (Don't confuse the last example with the possessive: *Beezus is Ramona's big sister.*)

All in all, contractions are pretty slick. They're neat time savers, like microwaves and calculators. But contractions aren't modern inventions. People have been shrinking words ever since English was born more than a thousand years ago. In fact, some contractions are so ancient that we hardly hear them anymore. They've retired and gone to live in the word museum. Among them are *mayn't* (short for "may not"), *shan't* (short for "shall not"), *'tis* ("it is"), *'twas* ("it was"), *'twill* ("it will"), *'twould* ("it would"), and even the three-in-one wonder *'twon't* ("it will not").

So don't let anybody tell you that contractions are some kind of newfangled slang. They have a long, honorable history.

Still, not every contraction is acceptable English. Some words just don't get along well together. Here's the nitty-gritty on contractions that are respectable and those that get no respect at all.

The Respectables

aren't	are not	I've	I have
can't	cannot	isn't	is not
couldn't	could not	it'll	it will
didn't	did not	it's	it is;
doesn't	does not		it has
don't	do not	let's	let us
hadn't	had not	mightn't	might not
hasn't	has not	mustn't	must not
haven't	have not	oughtn't	ought not
he'd	he would;	she'd	she would;
	he had		she had
he'll	he will	she'll	she will
he's	he is;	she's	she is;
	he has		she has
here's	here is	shouldn't	should not
I'd	I would;	that's	that is;
	I had		that has
I'll	I will	there's	there is;
I'm	I am		there has

70

they'd	they would; they had	what've	what have
		where's	where is
they'll	they will	who'd	who would; who had
they're	they are		
they've	they have	who'll	who will
wasn't	was not	who's	who is; who has
we'd	we would; we had		
		who've	who have
we'll	we will	won't	will not
we're	we are	wouldn't	would not
we've	we have	you'd	you would; you had
weren't	were not		
what'll	what will	you'll	you will
what're	what are	you're	you are
what's	what is; what has	you've	you have

The Disreputables

• **ain't.** It's not OK, and it never will be. It's not standard English, so if you want to sound educated, don't use *ain't* unless you're trying to be funny. Use *am not* or a legitimate contraction like *isn't* or *aren't* instead. Still, *ain't* has one redeeming quality. It rhymes with lots of stuff.

The Taint of Ain't

I have a complaint about the word *ain't*.
It has rotten manners and no self-restraint.
Each time that I hear it, I start to feel faint.
No matter who says it, good English it *ain't*.

• **could've, should've, would've, might've, must've.** These are clumsy and awkward in writing. Spell them out: *could have, should have, would have,* and so on. (Grammatical horrors like *could of, should of,* and *would of* are even worse. See page 98.)

• **gonna, gotta, wanna.** Ugh! These aren't contractions, they're crimes in progress. They may be fine in an instant message to a friend, but when your English should be its best, write them out: *going to, got to, want to.*

• **how'd, how'll, how're, how's, when'll, when're, when's, where'd, where'll, where're, why'd, why're, why's.** Don't form contractions with *how, when, where,* or *why* (except for that old standby *where's*). We all say things like, "*How'm* I supposed to get there?" and "*Where're* my socks?" But don't put them in writing. Spell them out.

• **it'd, that'd, there'd, this'd, what'd.** These aren't valid, either. Write them at your peril.

• **that'll, that're, that've, there'll, there're, there've, this'll.** Ditto. Avoid at all costs when you're writing.

> **Note** Don't add *at* to *where's* or *where is.*
> Wrong: *Where's Waldo at?*
> Right: *Where's Waldo?*

CASTING A SPELL
How to Be Letter Perfect

Contrary to popular opinion, your spell-checker does not know how to spell. It doesn't care whether someone's a *guerrilla* or a *gorilla*, whether he lives in a *desert* or a *dessert*, or whether he has a *sweet* tooth or a *suite* tooth. It can't choose between similar words and doesn't care which one you use. It's not picky.

Humans, however, are picky. They notice the differences between words that sound alike (*way* and *weigh*, for example, or *rain* and *reign*), and words that are similar but not the same (like *not* and *now*, or *affect* and *effect*, or *how* and *who*). To your spell-checker, one is just as good as another.

The lesson? Know how to spell, instead of expecting your computer to think for you. Sure, go ahead and use your spell-checker, but don't depend on it to catch every mistake. The truth is, your spell-

checker needs a spell-checker—and that's you! (The grammar-checker in your computer isn't any better. See page xviii.)

OK, it's rhyme time again. Your spell-checker won't find the mistakes in this poem, but I'll bet you can.

Moose Takes

When you write that chocolate moose is suite
And poems are red allowed,
That polar bares have dancing feat
And reign was ones a cloud,

When you say for pears add up to ate,
And wails swim in the see,
You can fool the spelling-checker,
But you can't fool little me.

Try making up a poem of your own to fool the spell-checker. Who would have thought that spelling could be fun? With the right attitude, you'll find that even hard words are easy to learn. Here's a list of some tricky ones, with tips to help the spellbound.

• **accept / except.** To *accept* something is to take it or agree to it. *Except* means "other than." *"I never* **accept** *attachments," said Buffy, "**except** the ones I get from Willow."*

• **accidentally.** No, it's not spelled "accidently." There's an "ally" at the end. *The Baudelaires needed an ally when they **accidentally** encountered an unfortunate event.*

• **affect / effect.** The action word (the verb) is *affect,* but the thing that results (the noun) is an *effect.* (There are rare exceptions, but we won't worry about them now.) *The virus did not **affect** Willow's computer, but it had a devastating **effect** on the attachments she sent.*

• **ain't.** You shouldn't be trying to spell this—it's a serious misdemeanor. (See pages 71-72.) *Paige **isn't** happy, Phoebe and Piper **aren't** speaking, and **I'm not** getting involved.*

• **all ready / already.** They're not the same. *All ready* means "prepared," but *already* means "previously." *Pete and Chloe are **all ready** to boogie. In fact, they've **already** started.*

• **all together / altogether.** *All together* means "all at once" or "all in one place." *The Weasleys were **all together** at Christmas. Altogether* means "in sum" or "entirely." ***Altogether** there were nine of them. Molly was **altogether** delighted.*

• **alot.** It's two words, not one. *Lex hasn't done **a lot** of good in his life.*

• **alright.** No, "alright" is not *all right*—it's all wrong! *"**All right**, I'll let you whitewash the fence," said Tom.*

• **anywheres.** Never use this anywhere. *"The demons could be almost **anywhere**," said Angel.*

• **arctic.** Yes, it's *arctic,* not "artic." And it's *Antarctica,* not "Antartica." *The **arctic** fox hangs out at the North Pole.* (A chilly riddle: Why is the word *arctic* like a piano? They both have a middle *c*.)

• **awesome.** Don't forget the *e* in the middle. *"These dangly earrings are awesome!" Paris said.*

• **believe.** It has *ie* in the middle, not *ei*. This is an example of the old "*i* before *e*, except after *c*" rule (see the box below). *If you **believe** in fairies, clap your hands!*

I Before E, Except After C

When I was in school, kids used to memorize this little rhyme:

> Use *i* before *e*, except after *c*,
> Or when sounded like *a*,
> As in *neighbor* and *weigh*.

I still use it to check my spelling when I come across words that have an *e* and an *i* next to each other. Even though it doesn't work a hundred percent of the time, it's a neat way to deal with a ticklish problem.

Of course, there are always weird words that don't cooperate. The most common exceptions to the rule (besides *weird* itself) are *either, foreign, height, leisure, neither, seize, sheik, species,* and *their.*

- **beside / besides.** *Beside* means "by the side of," and *besides* means "in addition." *Harry sat **beside** Ron on the train. He shared Ron's lunch and had a chocolate frog **besides**.*

- **capital / capitol.** If you mean the important city where lawmakers meet, use *capital*. If you mean the building they meet in, use *capitol*. *Denver, the **capital** of Colorado, has a **capitol** with a gold-plated dome.* Hint: A *capitol* usually has a *dome*, and both words have *o*'s. (As you might guess, a big letter is called a *capital* letter because it's important, like a *capital* city.)

- **definitely.** There is no *a* whatsoever. (Hint: It has "finite" in the middle.) *"These are **definitely** real diamonds," Paris said.*

- **desert / dessert.** The first is usually a hot and dry place. The second is the best part of dinner (the extra *s* is for "sweet"). *Willy has invented the perfect **dessert**: a chocolate ice cream that doesn't melt, even in the **desert**.*

- **dual / duel.** If you're a Jedi knight, you probably mean *duel*, the one with an *e*. *Luke was seriously injured in the **duel**.* The other word, *dual*, means "double." *Arnold's Harley has **dual** carburetors.*

- **embarrass.** Two *r*'s and two *s*'s. *Spock was not **embarrassed** by his pointy ears.*

- **emigrate / immigrate.** You *emigrate* <u>from</u> one country and *immigrate* <u>to</u> another. *Arnold **emigrated*** *from Austria in 1968. He became an American citizen in 1983, fifteen years after he* **immigrated** *to the United States.* Memory aid: *Emigrate* begins with *e*, like "exit," and *immigrate* begins with *i*, like "into."

• **excellent.** There's no *a*. *That Krabby Patty was* **excellent**!

• **gorilla / guerrilla.** The big ape is a *gorilla*. The other word, which refers to an unconventional warrior, has two *r*'s as well as two *l*'s. *A* **gorilla** *ate the* **guerrilla** *who was hiding in the jungle.*

• **grammar.** If you spell this with "er" at the end, give yourself an F! *Dale Jr. got a ticket from the* **grammar** *police.*

• **hear / here.** A trick for remembering: You *hear* with your *e-a-r*. *"I can't* **hear** *you from way over* **here**," *said Jody.*

• **hyper / hypo.** Added to the front of a word, *hyper* means "over" or "more"; *hypo* means "under" or "less." *Dudley becomes* **hyper***active and gets a rash if he doesn't use a* **hypo***allergenic soap.*

• **it's / its.** It's all explained on page 32.

• **know / no.** It's important to *know* the difference. *No* kidding!

• **lay / lie.** *Lay* means "place" or "put down." *Lie* means "recline." It helps to remember that *lay* sounds like "place" and *lie* sounds like "recline." For more, see page 60.

- **lightning.** There's an *e* in *thunder* but not in *lightning*. *Harry's scar looks like a **lightning** bolt.*

Memory Tricks

Do you have a hard time spelling the word *rhythm*? I used to, until Mrs. Trotter, my fourth-grade teacher, showed me a trick for remembering: **R**hythm **H**elps **Y**our **T**wo **H**ips **M**ove. The first letters spell *rhythm*. Pretty neat, huh? I never forgot again.

Something else I used to have trouble spelling was the name *Caesar*, as in Julius Caesar or Sid Caesar or caesar salad. So I made up a secret code of my own. What does *Caesar* have for breakfast? **C**heese **A**nd **E**ggs **S**erved **A**ll **R**unny.

You can play tricks like these, too. If a word is hard for you to spell, invent your own secret code. Make up a saying that will help you remember the letters.

What happens in the *ocean*?
Old **C**odfish **E**at **A**nd **N**ap.
What do you find *weird*?
Wild **E**lephants **I**n **R**ed **D**resses.

What do you *harass* a bully with?

Hexes **A**nd **R**ats **A**nd **S**limy **S**not!

What can you do to *seize* victory?

Stop **E**vil **I**n **Z**ombies **E**verywhere.

Don't worry about sounding silly. Your memory trick doesn't have to make sense. In fact, the sillier the better. What matters is that you can remember it when you need it.

• **necessary.** Use one *c* and two *s*'s. *Mary found it* ***necessary*** *to open her umbrella.*

• **nuclear.** Don't forget the *e* sound in the middle. The correct pronunciation is NOO-klee-ur (not NOO-kyoo-lur). *"My business is* ***nuclear*** *energy," said Homer.*

• **pore / pour.** You *pore* over an engrossing book, but it's gross to *pour* over one. *While Phoebe* ***pored*** *over a hot novel, the bathtub* ***poured*** *over.*

• **principal / principle.** A *principal* is a big shot (like the head of a school) and plays an important, or *principal*, role. A *principle*, on the other hand, is a rule (of conduct, morality, or nature, for example). *Mr. Skinner, the* ***principal****, says Bart has no* ***principles****.*

• **raise / rise.** See pages 60-61.

• **scissors.** It has four *s*'s, one at each end and two

in the middle. Count them! *"Don't run with **scissors**, Claudia," said Mrs. Frankweiler.*

• **separate.** It has two *a*'s (look for the "para" in the middle). *Each of the Halliwell sisters has her own **separate** paranormal powers.*

• **set / sit.** See pages 60-61.

• **spade / spayed.** A gardener with a *spade* likes to work in the shade. But a female pet is *spayed* by the vet. *Miss Kitty Fantastico, who was **spayed** last year, chewed the handle off Willow's **spade**.* (Note: *Spaded* means "used a spade," so save it for the garden, not the vet's.)

• **spoonful.** One *l* at the end. And the plural is *spoonfuls*. *Dweezil's recipe for peanut butter pizza calls for a **spoonful** of grape jelly and two **spoonfuls** of crunchy peanut butter.*

• **stationary / stationery.** If the *stationery* (paper) is *stationary* (fixed or still), you can write on it, and it won't move. (Hint: Both *stationery* and *paper* contain "er.") *"If you haven't become **stationary**, Butler, please get up and bring me my **stationery**," said Artemis.*

• **than / then.** If you're less than certain, then see page 102.

• **their / there / they're.** No, *they're* not the same, though *there* are many people who confuse them in *their* writing. For more, see pages 13 and 34.

• **to / too / two.** The shortest, *to*, is the one you see most often. You use it mainly to show directions or locations. *Clark went **to** the Talon and sat next **to** Lana.* Sometimes *to* is used with an action word, or verb. *Clark offered **to** fix the leaky pipe.* The *too* with double *o*'s means "extremely" or "also." *Clark was **too** fast for Lana. She missed seeing him weld the pipe and use his superpowers, **too**.* Finally, *two* is what you get when you add one plus one. *The **two** of them drank iced tea and did their homework.* For more, see page 104.

• **toward.** This is the preferred American spelling, with no *s* at the end. The same goes for *afterward, backward, downward, forward, onward,* and *upward*—no *s* needed. *Zack and Cody were last seen heading **toward** the elevator.*

• **who's / whose.** See page 33.

• **you're / your.** See page 34.

CAPITAL CRIMES
When Size Matters

Question: What poet is like a capital letter?

Answer: Longfellow.

Question: When does a small letter borrow money?

Answer: When he finds himself short.

Enough silliness. Now here's a question that's not a riddle. Why do we need both capital letters (LIKE THESE) and small letters (like these)?

As with most things, there's a reason. A capital letter here and there makes reading easier by telling us where sentences begin and which words are special. When something is written in all small letters or all big ones, we have to concentrate harder and figure those things out for ourselves. Who needs the eyestrain and the headaches?

I know what you're thinking. If we're supposed to use both big letters and small ones, why do we see so many things that are written all one way or the other?

Well, cartoon characters (like the ones in this book) get to talk in capital letters. Don't ask me why—it's a cartoon thing. As for everybody else, some people are sloppy, others are clueless, and still others are trying to be quick or cute or cool (say, in e-mails or instant messages). But if we all wrote that way all the time, reading would be a lot harder (and boring, too).

Now, you don't have to be letter perfect if you're IM-ing your best friend. But when your writing really counts, don't forget to use capital letters and small ones. Think of the reader when you write! Here's the scoop on how to use big and little letters.

INITIAL PUBLIC OFFERING

We use capital letters to start a new sentence, like the one you're reading now. The next one begins with a capital letter, too. So do all the others in this paragraph. That makes reading much, much easier. Why? Because the capital letters make strings of words look more organized and less like a plate of spaghetti.

NAME-DROPPING

Capital letters are used to begin the names of people and pets to show that they're special words: *Ashton, Lindsay, and Orlando, along with the Talbots' dog, Wishbone, were guests of Oprah Winfrey.*

Names (like *Joe* and *Wishbone*) are called proper nouns. The ordinary words for these (*boy* and *dog*) are called common nouns, and they begin with small letters. (Slip a little noun sense into your conversation sometime and wow your parents.)

I SPY

I, another special word, is always capitalized. How's that for a self-esteem builder! *"I believe that I am worthy of a capital letter at all times," said Angelica.*

Why do we capitalize *I* and not *you* or *they* or *he* or *she*? It's true that *I* is an important word, but that's not the reason. Without high heels, shy little *i* would be hard to see and might get lost in the shuffle. See what i mean?

LOCATION, LOCATION, LOCATION

The names of places—like cities, states, countries, even planets—start with capital letters. *On his days off, Kirk can beam himself to Hoboken or Hawaii or Mordor or Vulcan.* If the name has two parts, we capitalize both. *He's already been to St. Louis, South America, Middle Earth, and Alpha Centauri.*

You remember what special names like these are called, don't you? Yes, they're proper nouns.

THE DATING GAME

We use capital letters to begin the names of days (like *Friday* or *Saturday*), months (say, *June, July,* or *August*), and holidays (*Thanksgiving* or *Mother's Day*). *Miss Piggy reminded Kermit that Valentine's Day fell on the second Monday in February.*

EDIFICE COMPLEX

The names of buildings (the *Pentagon* or *Tintagel Castle,* for instance) and events (the *Olympics,* the *Trojan War*) also start with capital letters. *William Barfee was too sick to attend the Putnam County Spelling Bee at Lake Hemingway–Dos Passos Junior High.*

STREET SMARTS

If our houses and other buildings didn't have addresses, we'd get lost all the time. In fact, addresses are so important that each word in them begins with a capital letter. *Fala, Barney, and Miss Beazley are famous Scotties who have lived at 1600 Pennsylvania Avenue, Washington, D.C.* (If you don't want to spell out *Avenue* or *Street* or *Road* in an address, you can use *Ave.* or *St.* or *Rd.*)

TITLE TALES

If someone is entitled to a title, the title is entitled to a capital letter. So we use capital letters to begin the titles of folks like *General* Grievous, *Principal* Snyder, *Doctor* Watson, *Queen* Jadis, *President* Bartlet, *Professor* Von Drake, and *Commander* Root. *Entering the royal chamber, Sir Gawaine approached King Arthur, who sat with Queen Guenever on one side and Sir Lancelot on the other.*

We begin *Mr., Ms., Miss,* and *Mrs.* with capital letters because they're titles too (we call them courtesy titles). Words like *aunt, uncle, grandfather,* and *grandma* are also titles when they come in front of names, as in *Uncle* Fester and *Grandma* Ingalls. *After Mr. and Mrs. Trotter were killed in a rhinoceros accident, James went to live with Aunt Sponge and Aunt Spiker.*

We also capitalize *aunt, uncle,* and the rest when we speak or write to a relative ("Let me help, *Grandma,*" or "Hi, *Uncle*"). Otherwise, words for relatives start with small letters. *James went to live with his two aunts.*

SHORTCUTS

An abbreviation, the shortened form of a word or phrase, is a handy little thing that makes life easier. When it's not necessary to spell out a long word or phrase, you can use a letter or two to do the job.

We use capital letters for initials (as in *J. K.* Rowling or *C. S.* Lewis) and other abbreviations (like *AC* for "air-conditioning," *IM* for "instant message," and *DJ* for "disc jockey"). That way, we don't have to write everything out. What a time saver! *When the babysitter fell asleep, Stewie turned up the AC and sent an IM to his favorite DJ.*

You've probably noticed that some short-cuts have both large and small letters (like *Dr.* and *St.*) while others have only capitals (say, *MD*). Here's why. When we abbreviate a single word (like "Doctor" or "Street" in a name or address), only the first letter is capitalized. But when we abbreviate two or more words (like "Medical Doctor"), we use all capitals— one for each important word. *Dr. John H. Watson, an eminent MD, called on Sherlock Holmes at 221B Baker St.*

You may also have noticed that some abbreviations have dots and some don't. If you're not sure, check the dictionary. For more about the dotty stuff, see Chapter 10.

PRODUCT UPDATES

The names of companies (like *Kellogg's* or *General Mills*) and the things they make (*Froot Loops* or *Lucky Charms*) are usually capitalized. *Ashley and Mary-Kate had Egg McMuffins for breakfast at McDonald's, and Double Whoppers for lunch at Burger King.*

Of course, some companies, like eBay, and some products, like iPod, just have to be different. They deliberately break the rules to catch our attention.

GROUP THERAPY

We use big letters for the important words in the names of institutions (schools, libraries, churches, and hospitals, for instance) and groups (like clubs, political parties, and religions). *Fred and Barney belong to the Loyal Order of Water Buffaloes. Jane is giving a speech to the Galaxy Women Historical Society about a Baptist settlement on Saturn.*

NAME THAT TUNE

My nephew Craig can read *The Lord of the Rings* while he listens to Green Day, plays Nintendogs, and watches "Drake & Josh." You're probably a multitasker, too, but do you know why there are so many big letters in that sentence?

There's a reason, of course. We use capital letters to begin the important words in the titles of books and the names of musical groups, video games, and television shows. The same goes for creative works like songs, paintings, and poems. (In fact, each line of a poem can start with a capital letter, even if it's not a complete sentence.)

You may have wondered why some titles, like *Huckleberry Finn*, usually appear in slanting (or italic) letters while others, like "The Star-Spangled Banner," usually appear in ordinary type surrounded by those little thingies called quotation marks.

Customs vary on how titles should be written. Here's the usual practice. The names of longer works, like books, movies, and plays, usually are printed in italic letters. The names of smaller works, like songs, poems, stories, paintings, and TV shows, usually go in ordinary type with quotation marks. There's more about quotation marks in Chapter 10.

CHAPTER 9

ENDANGERED LIST
The Bruised, the Abused, and the Misused

Language is a lot like a gory video game. Words bravely soldier on for ages, battling the forces of abuse and neglect. Some fall facedown in the trenches, their original meanings lost after years of mistreatment. Others overcome incredible odds and survive with barely a scratch.

Still others are the walking wounded, words misused so often that they're in danger of losing their meaning. Bloodied but unbowed, these endangered words shouldn't be given up for dead. Fortunately, it's not too late to save them. Give them back their true identities and they'll live to fight another day.

Here's a list of words that need our help. It's a dangerous mission, but somebody's got to do it!

• **among / between.** Use *between* when two are involved, and *among* for three or more. *A disagreement **between** Tibby and Lena created conflict **among** the four girls in the sisterhood.*

• **bad / badly**. Many adults get these mixed up, too. Use *badly* to talk about what someone or something actively does—like behave. *Smeagol behaved **badly**.* Use *bad* to talk about the condition that someone or something is in—how he looks or feels or smells, perhaps. *Afterward, Smeagol looked **bad**, he felt **bad**, and he even smelled **bad**.* (If you said *Smeagol looked **badly**,* you'd mean he didn't see well. Maybe Smeagol needs glasses.)

- **bad / worse / worst.** When something is more than *bad*, it's *worse*. When something is as *bad* as it can be, it's the *worst*. Use *worse* to compare one thing with another, and *worst* to compare one thing with two or more. *Your dog is **bad** but mine is **worse**. In fact, mine is the **worst** in the obedience class.* (No, "badder" and "baddest" won't do!) For more about comparing things, see pages 97 and 100.

- **bring / take.** Which way is the stuff moving? Is it coming or going? If it's coming toward you, someone's *bringing* it. If it's going away from you, then someone's *taking* it. *"**Bring** me my dessert," said Stewie, "and **take** away these vegetables!"* But what if you're the one carrying the stuff? Are you *bringing* it or are you *taking* it? It all depends on which end of the journey you're talking about. If you're talking about where the stuff is coming from, you're *taking* it. *I'm **taking** you from the dragon.* If you're talking about where the stuff is going, you're *bringing* it. *Lord Farquaad wants me to **bring** you to him.*

- **can / may.** No, you may not use these interchangeably. If you *can* do something, you're "able to," but if you *may*, you're "permitted to." *Opal's dad says she **may** keep the dog if she **can** take care of it.* For more, see pages 61-62.

How Cool Is Cool?

Cool is a cool word, but it's not always cool enough. When something is more than cool, it's *cooler*. When it's the most cool of all, it's the *coolest*.

We use *er* words like *cooler* to compare one thing with another. We use *est* words like *coolest* to compare one thing with two or more. *A sub is **cooler** than a cheeseburger, but a burrito is the **coolest** of them all.*

I think I've finally figured out
The point of *er* and *est.*
It's how we make comparisons,
In case you haven't guessed.

With two things, use an *er* word.
With three things, use an *est.*
That's how *good* gets *better,*
And *better* becomes *best.*

For more about comparing things, see pages 96 and 100-101.

• **could of / should of / would of.** These are serious misdemeanors. We often pronounce *could have*, *should have*, and *would have* as though the *h* in *have* were silent. That's OK in speech, but don't forget the *have* when you write. Spell it out! For more, see page 72.

• **etc.** This abbreviation (short for *et cetera*) means "and other things." Since "and" is already part of the package, don't say "and *etc.*" And since "other" is already there, too, it's redundant (that is, unnecessary) to say "etc., etc." Once is enough. *The witches' brew contained a frog's toe, a newt's eye, a lizard's leg, an owl's wing, etc.*

Is That an Eyeball or a Bellybutton?

Sometimes it's the little things that trip us up—like those pipsqueaks *a* and *an*. How do you decide which one to put in front of a word?

Usually, the choice is obvious: we say **an** *eyeball*, not **a** *eyeball*, and **a** *bellybutton*, not **an** *bellybutton*. This is because we use *an* with "soft" sounds (like the *e* in *eyeball*) and *a* with "hard" sounds (like the *b* in *bellybutton*). Things are easier to pronounce this way.

The letters of the alphabet come in two varieties, soft-sounding and hard-sounding. The soft letters—*a, e, i, o,* and *u*—are called vowels. The hard letters—*b, c, d, f, g, h, j, k, l, m, n, p, q, r, s, t, v, w, x, y,* and *z*—are called consonants. This is useful information to know in case you're ever on "Wheel of Fortune."

Now back to *a* and *an.* Most of the time, we use *a* in front of a vowel, or soft letter, and *an* in front of a consonant, or hard one. But some letters have split personalities, like Dr. Jekyll and Mr. Hyde.

The letter *h* is officially a hard letter, but it sometimes acts like a soft one. And *u* is officially a soft letter, but it sometimes acts like a hard one. What's more, *e* and *u* are soft letters that sound hard when mushed together at the beginning of a word.

OK, don't hyperventilate. This isn't as tough as it looks. Here's what to put in front of a word that starts with *h* or *u* or *eu:*

- Use *an* before a silent *h* (as in *heir, hour, honor,* and *herbal*). No, most Americans don't pronounce the *h* in *herbal.*
- Use *a* before the *h* that you can hear

(the *ha-ha* variety, as in *hero, history, hotel, hula,* and *hyena*).

- Use *an* before a *u* that sounds like "uh" (as in *umbrella, umpire, uncle, underwear,* and *uptight*).
- Use *a* before a *u* that sounds like "you" (as in *unicorn, unique, unisex, uranium,* and *utopia*).
- Use *a* before *eu,* which also sounds like "you" (as in *eulogy, euphemism, euphoria, eureka,* and *European*).

• **fewer / less.** Lots of people have forgotten (or never learned) that there's a difference between *fewer* and *less.* They rely on *less* for all occasions. That doesn't mean you should. Use *fewer* for a smaller number of individual things, and *less* for a smaller amount of one thing. *The **fewer** passengers Herbie carries, the **less** gas he uses.*

• **gonna / gotta / wanna.** You've got to be kidding! See page 73.

• **good / better / best.** When something is more than *good,* it's *better.* When something is as *good* as it can be, it's the *best.* Use *better* to compare one thing with another, and *best* to compare one thing with two or more. *My cat is **good** but yours is **better**. Yours is the **best** in the cat show.* (Need I say it? "Gooder" and "goodest" are not allowed.) For more about comparing things, see pages 96 and 97.

• **good / well.** These two give people fits. Use *well* to talk about what someone or something actively does. *Frodo behaved **well**.* Use *good* to talk about the condition that someone or something is in—how he looks or feels or smells, for instance. *Afterward, Frodo looked **good**, he felt **good**, and he even smelled **good**.* If you're talking about Frodo's physical health, however, you may use either *well* or *good*, though *well* is clearer. *Despite his wounds, Frodo looked **well** and felt **well**.*

• **inside.** It doesn't need help, so don't attach an unnecessary "of," as in "inside of his shirt." *Ron keeps Scabbers **inside** his shirt.*

• **it's / its.** See page 32.

• **like.** *Like* is a cool word. In one sense, it means "similar to," so it's handy for comparing things. And as a verb, it means to be fond of someone or something. I like *like*! But it's possible to like *like* a little too much. You probably know what's coming. Many kids (even some adults) incessantly say "I'm *like*" instead of "I said," and "He's *like*" instead of "He said." *My teacher's **like**, "Meg, how can you be such a poor student?"* This informal way of using *like* is fine for talking to your friends. But when you're writing or giving a speech or talking to the Prince of Wales, you'd better get out your best English. This means using a word such as *say* or *said*, not *like*, to quote somebody. *My teacher said, "Meg, how can you be such a poor student?"*

• **off.** This word doesn't need help. So don't attach an unnecessary "of," as in "off of his dragon." *Eragon was knocked off his dragon, Saphira.*

• **than / then.** Use *than* when you're comparing things, like two sisters: *Britney is older than Jamie Lynn.* Use *then* when something comes after or is caused by something else: *The sisters bought a Lexus, then gave it to their mom for Mother's Day.* For advice on using *I* or *me* after *than*, see pages 11-13.

The Which Trials

Are you spooked by *which*es? Well, who isn't? Everybody is haunted at one time or another by the problem of choosing between *that* and *which*.

Let's see if you can pick the right sentence:

♦ *Only ghosts, **which** have heads, can wear hats.*
♦ *Only ghosts **that** have heads can wear hats.*

If you picked No. 2 (*Only ghosts **that** have heads can wear hats*), give yourself a pat on the head. Here's what to ask yourself before choosing *which* or *that*. Is the *which* or the *that* and the stuff attached to it (in this case ***which** have heads* or ***that** have heads*) vital information?

If the answer is no, use *which*.

If the answer is yes, use *that*.

Look again at the correct sentence: *Only ghosts **that** have heads can wear hats*. Without the vital information (***that** have heads*), the sentence would say, *Only ghosts can wear hats*. This isn't what you mean. It's not even true. You and I can wear hats, and we're not ghosts. Without the crucial stuff, the sentence goes poof!

OK, that's *that*. Now let's see a *which* at work.

*Headless ghosts, **which** don't need hats, are scary.*

Why is that sentence correct? Because we use *which* for information that isn't vital. If you dumped *which* and the stuff attached to it (*don't need hats*), you'd still make your point: *Headless ghosts are scary.*

The missing information is interesting, but it's not vital.

If you're very observant, you've noticed that *which* information is surrounded by commas, like this, but *that* information isn't. Remember this the next time you're haunted by *which*es:

Commas, *which* cut out the fat,

Go with *which*, never with *that*.

For more on *which* and *that*, see pages 64-65 and 110.

their / there / they're. See pages 13-14, 34, and 83.

to / too / two. Here they are in action: *After I played Warcraft for **two** hours it was **too** late **to** study, so I went **to** bed.* For more on these three, see page 84.

The Incomparable Unique

If it's *unique*, it's the one and only. It's unparalleled, without equal, incomparable, unrivaled, one of a kind. In other words, there's nothing like it—anywhere.

Something either is or is not *unique*.

It can't be more, less, sort of, rather, very, quite, slightly, especially, absolutely, positively, somewhat, or particularly *unique*. Why? Because the word *unique* stands alone.

*Alice's looking glass is **unique**.*

who's / whose. See page 33.
you're / your. See page 34.

Before we leave the endangered list, here's a reminder about *a* and *an*, two common species that are often confused when they come before a word beginning with *h*. In case you've forgotten how to use them, see pages 98-100.

The Nose Knows

A hero full of mystery
Fell ill at *a* hotel.
His nostrils had *a* history
Of making him unwell.

An heir who was *an* honest chap
Then helpfully suggested:
"*An* hour in *an* herbal wrap
Will get you decongested."

CONNECTING THE DOTS
All About Punctuation

I'll bet you've met Mr. Smiley :-) and Mr. Frownie :-(and all the other cute guys that illustrate the moods of people who message each other online. And I'll bet you've noticed that these sideways faces are made up of the same little things—we call them punctuation marks—that help us organize our writing.

When punctuation marks aren't busy making faces, they have an important job to do. They're the signs, signals, and other aids that help direct traffic when we write. Like road signs, they tell us where to stop, start, slow down, and make detours.

A lot of people seem to think that punctuation isn't really necessary. Think again, people! Without it, life could get very messy. If you don't believe me, consider this sentence: *Cora said John is acting silly.*

The meaning is obvious, right? But add some punctuation and the sentence means something

entirely different: *"Cora," said John, "is acting silly."*

See what I mean, silly? In the first sentence, John is the silly one. In the second, it's Cora. What a difference a few punctuation marks can make!

If you were reading those two sentences aloud, you'd make them sound different. (Try it and see.) That's because when you talk, your voice puts in stops and starts and pauses to show how the words go together and what the sentence means.

When you write, you need a way to show where the stops and starts and pauses go. That's what punctuation marks are for.

The traffic signs and signals that we see on the road aren't hard to understand, and neither are the aids we use in our writing. Let's take a look at them, one mark at a time.

END OF THE ROAD

The Period

The period is the stop sign at the end of a sentence. When you reach the period, the sentence is finished. If you have anything else to say, you start a new sentence.

An ordinary sentence—one that states rather than asks or exclaims—always ends with a period. *Eloise loves the glittering windows at Tiffany & Company.*

If there's already a dot at the end (for example, when the sentence ends with an abbreviation like *etc.* or *St.* or *Co.*), don't add another. *Eloise loves the glittering windows at Tiffany & Co.*

Some abbreviations have dots and some don't. Check the dictionary if you're not sure. For more about abbreviations, see pages 90-91.

UNCOMMONLY USEFUL

The Comma

A comma is like a yellow light that helps prevent pileups at a busy corner. It organizes words in much the same way that the yellow light keeps traffic moving in an orderly fashion. Ignore a comma, and you risk a fender-bender in your writing!

Yeah, yeah, I hear you saying. How can something so tiny and innocent-looking be so important? Well, just look at these two sentences. Add one little comma, and the sentence changes completely:

> *Harriet quit saying she would give up spying.*
>
> *Harriet quit, saying she would give up spying.*

In the first sentence, Harriet stops talking about quitting. In the second, she actually quits. The lesson? Ignore commas at your peril! Here's how to use them.

To separate a series of things, names, or actions. *Harriet's spy tools included a flashlight, a Boy Scout knife, a water canteen, a notebook, and pens. She eavesdropped on Mr. Waldenstein, Mr. Hanley, and Mrs. McNair. She climbed a tree, lurked on a rooftop, peered through a window, and scribbled in her notebook.*

To call people by name. *Harriet, come down from the roof and get ready for dinner.* Or: *Come down from the roof and get ready for dinner, Harriet.* Or: *Come down from the roof, Harriet, and get ready for dinner.* Note that you need only one comma if the name begins or ends the sentence, but two if it's in the middle.

To quote people. The comma can go after the quotation: *"I'll be down in a minute," Harriet said.* Or it can come before the quotation: *Harriet said, "I'll be down in a minute."* The same rule applies if you're not using quotation marks. *Harriet asked herself, Where did I put my flashlight?* (Whether or not you use quotation marks, you don't need a comma after a question mark or an exclamation point. *Did it roll off the roof? she wondered. "Oh, here it is!" she shouted.*)

To set apart opening words. *As usual, she put her extra pens in the leather case. Of course, she kept her favorite pen with her notebook.* You can skip the comma, though, when you don't want to stress the opening words.

To surround information that interrupts a sentence. *Her favorite pen, the blue one with yellow stripes, was a gift from Golly.* For other ways to set apart an interruption, see pages 114-117.

To tie "mini-sentences" together. *Harriet put the notebook in her underwear drawer, and she joined her parents at the dinner table.* You need both a comma and a connecting word, like *and* or *but*, to link "mini-sentences" (they're officially called clauses). A clause is easy to recognize because it has its own subject and verb. For another way to combine these "mini-sentences," see the next page.

To surround *which* information. *Harriet returned to her room, which was on the third floor, after finishing dinner.* For more about commas and *which*, see page 104.

THE PAUSE THAT REFRESHES

The Semicolon

If the period is a stop sign and the comma is a yellow light, then the semicolon is a flashing red, one of those lights you go through after a brief pause. It's for times when you want something stronger than a comma but not quite so final as a period.

Unfortunately, people tend to forget about the semicolon when they write, even people who would never ignore a flashing red light on the road. What a shame! Here's how to use this handy punctuation mark.

To tie "mini-sentences" together without a connecting word. *The March girls lived at home with their mother; their father was away at war.* A "mini-sentence" (a clause, remember?) has its own subject and verb. For another way to join clauses, see the previous page.

To clear up a confusing series. *The party included Jo, who poured the tea; her mother, Marmee; John Brooke, the tutor; Laurie; Meg, who baked the cookies; and the other March girls.* Imagine that sentence with all commas and no semicolons. If you didn't know who everybody was, you might think that Jo's mother and Marmee were two different people, and that Laurie was the tutor instead of John.

INTRODUCTORY REMARKS
The Colon

Think of the colon as a traffic cop that pulls you over to warn you about travel conditions up ahead. It's an abrupt stop that's almost like a period. A colon makes you hit the brakes before it introduces something else. Here's how to use one.

To introduce a long quotation. *Peter said to Edmund: "I hurt my arm. I don't think it's broken, but it might be sprained. If you put a bandage on it, I can go on dueling."* If the quotation is short, only a sentence or so, you can use a comma instead of a colon. See pages 109-110.

To introduce a list. *Peter and Edmund changed back into their school uniforms: jackets, pants, ties, and caps.* But use a colon only if the introductory stuff could stand alone and be a sentence all by itself.

To explain or expand on a statement. *The children found themselves back where their adventure began: on a bench in a railroad station, surrounded by luggage.*

To tell time. *Edmund looked at the station clock. It was 2:37 PM, and his train was due at 3:10.* As you can see, the colon separates the hour from the minutes.

You don't need one when you write the hour alone. *He should arrive at school by 4:30 or 5.*

TO BE, OR NOT TO BE

The Question Mark

When you ask for directions, the question mark is the raised eyebrow at the end of your sentence. *Is this the way to Tara, Captain Short?* You use it to ask a question, of course, but also to show skepticism or surprise. *You're going to Tara, Commander Root? You really want to face that mob scene?*

That sounds simple, and most of the time, it is. But what do you do when a sentence continues after the question? First, end the question with a question mark, and then end the sentence itself with a period. *What's the fastest way to reach the LEPrecon unit? she wondered.* For more about question marks, see pages 110, 115, and 120.

ATTENTION GETTERS

!

The Exclamation Point

An exclamation point is like the horn on your car, something that shouts to get attention. *These vomit-flavored jelly beans are disgusting!*

If you shout too often, people will stop paying attention. So be sure to use exclamation points only when you have to. And when you do need to shout, use exclamation points one at a time. *Yuck!* (Not "Yuck!!!")

Now, what do you do when a sentence continues after an exclamation? First, end the shouted stuff with an exclamation point, then end the sentence itself with a period. *These earwax-flavored jelly beans are even worse! Nigel thought.* For more about exclamation points, see pages 110, 115, and 120.

SIDE TRIPS
( )
Parentheses

Sometimes you need to make a detour in your writing, an interruption to tuck information into a sentence or between sentences.

One way to signal this brief side trip is with parentheses, those marks that look like a frown and a smile if you turn your head sideways. A single one is called a parenthesis (the end rhymes with "hiss") and two are parentheses (the end rhymes with "cheese"). Hey, you just saw some of them in action!

The thing to know about parentheses is that they can enclose something within a sentence (like this), or they can enclose a sentence that stands alone. (This is the kind of sentence I mean.)

The tricky part of using parentheses is in figuring out where to put the other punctuation marks, like periods, commas, and question marks. Should they go inside or outside the ending parenthesis? (They never go in front of a beginning parenthesis.) Here's what to remember.

When the detour stands alone. Start the detour with a capital letter and put the final punctuation inside the parentheses. *Encyclopedia Brown's dad was the chief of police in Idaville. (He was Chief Brown's secret weapon.)*

When the detour is within a sentence. Start the detour with a small letter and put the punctuation outside the parentheses. *Leroy's nickname was Encyclopedia (he had a head full of facts).*

Exception: If the remark inside the parentheses is an exclamation *(wow!)* or a question *(huh?)*, the exclamation point or question mark goes inside the parentheses; any other punctuation marks go outside.

TOO MUCH OF A GOOD THING

The Dash

I'm tired of seeing so many dashes. We could do with a lot fewer. These days, the dash is probably more in your face than the overused exclamation point—and I admit to being an offender myself. (Oops, there I go again.)

The dash is like a detour sign; it interrupts the sentence and inserts another thought. One dash can be used in place of a colon to emphasize a piece of information. *It was what Dorothy dreaded most—a cyclone.* Or dashes can be used in pairs, like parentheses, to enclose a little side trip. *The house whirled around two or three times—Dorothy wasn't sure how many—then rose in the air like a balloon.*

There's nothing wrong with using a dash or two in your writing. But don't overdo it. Poor writers think they can get away with sticking dashes in whenever they don't know which punctuation marks to use. The result is a boring or confusing sentence.

Whether you're a certified dash addict or just a moderate abuser, get a grip.

Use no more than two per sentence. And if you do use two, they should surround a piece of information that interrupts the sentence. *The Wicked Witch of the East was killed—only her silver shoes were left—when Dorothy's house landed on her.*

If parentheses or commas would work as well, use them once in a while. *The Munchkins were grateful (they were free from bondage) and showed Dorothy the way to the Emerald City. They said Oz, the great Wizard who lived there, might help her get back to Kansas.*

Be careful not to confuse dashes with hyphens. The dash is longer than the little hyphen, which is used to connect words or parts of words (like *half-hour* and *ex-president*). For more about hyphens, see pages 21-22.

TO HAVE AND TO HAVE NOT
9
The Apostrophe

There's a little mark that hangs inside some words, including last names like O'Conner (yes, mine). As you go down the road, it's everywhere—on store awnings and windows, on the sides of trucks and buses, on billboards and electric signs. You see it every time you go to a McDonald's or a Wendy's.

That inescapable mark (it looks like a tiny 9 with the hole filled in) is an apostrophe. You pronounce that by emphasizing the "pos" and saying the *e* at the end. It sounds like "uh-PAH-struh-fee" and rhymes, more or less, with "catastrophe."

The poor apostrophe is one of the most mistreated punctuation marks. People insist on putting it in the wrong place at the wrong time. Let's call in the SPCA, the Society for the Prevention of Cruelty to Apostrophes, and end the abuse. Here's how apostrophes ought to be used.

To show who owns what. You can turn a word into a possessive by adding either an apostrophe alone or an apostrophe plus the letter *s*. If the word is singular (like *Opal* or *Otis*), add '*s*. ***Opal's*** *dog went to work with her in **Otis's** pet shop.* If the word is plural and ends in *s* (*animals*, for example), add the apostrophe alone. *The **animals'** cages stood empty as Otis serenaded the pets with his guitar.* If the word is plural but doesn't end in *s* (like *children*), add '*s*. *The **children's** arms were wrapped around Winn-Dixie.*

There's more about apostrophes and possessive words on pages 30-32.

To combine two words into one. An apostrophe shows where letters are dropped when words (like *could not*) are squashed into a contraction (like *couldn't*). *Opal **couldn't** find Winn-Dixie anywhere.* For more about contractions, see Chapter 6.

To make a single letter plural. Many people use apostrophes to make plural letters easier to read. *Opal never gets **A's** in spelling. Yesterday she forgot one of the **s's** in scissors.* For more about making single letters plural, see page 23.

SAYING IS BELIEVING
66 99
Quotation Marks

Quotation marks are like the road signs you see when you enter and leave a city. Just as the signs define the city limits, quotation marks show where speech begins and ends.

The quotation marks at the beginning (") look like a tiny 66 with the holes filled in. The quotation marks at the end (") look like a tiny 99 with the holes filled in. It helps to remember that 66 comes before 99. Here's how quotation marks work.

> *"You two are going be roommates," Danny announced.*
> *"So I can wear all D.J.'s clothes!" said Stephanie.*
> *"You mean I have to share my room with her?" D.J. asked.*

The opening quotation marks always go right in front of the first word. *"Come on, let's see some smiles,"*

Danny said. The trick is at the other end, where the closing quotation marks go. What do you do if there's another punctuation mark, like a period or a comma or a question mark? Does it go inside the closing quotation marks, or outside? That depends. Here's what's in and what's out.

Periods and commas go <u>inside</u> quotation marks. *"It's going to be just like a slumber party," Danny said. "We'll have lots of fun."*

Colons and semicolons go <u>outside</u> quotation marks. *Uncle Jesse has two recordings of "Blue Suede Shoes": one by Elvis and one by Carl Perkins. His favorite songs are "Love Me Tender," "Heartbreak Hotel," and "Hound Dog"; he's heard them thousands of times.*

Question marks and exclamation points usually go <u>inside</u> quotation marks. *"Hey, Uncle Jesse!" said Stephanie. "Can we play ballerina?"*

Exception: A question mark or an exclamation point goes outside quotation marks if it's not part of the quotation. This happens, for example, when a sentence includes a title that's inside quotation marks, like the name of a TV show, a radio program, or a song. *Who was Jesse's cohost on "Rush Hour Renegades"? It was Joey, otherwise known as "Ranger Joe"!*

A Walk in the Park

As I was strolling through the park
I came upon a question mark.
"How are you?" it said to me.
"What time is it? And where are we?"

Farther on I heard a yelp;
An exclamation point cried, "Help!"
I set off in a hasty dash—
But quickly halted, feeling rash.

Then I spied a pair of commas
Resting, briefly, in pajamas.
Suddenly I felt a breeze
(Surrounded by parentheses).

Above me, an apostrophe
Declared, "I'm hiding in a tree."
I climbed the branches to the top
Until a period said, "Stop."

CHAPTER 11

TALES FROM THE CRYPT
Clichés That Just Won't Die

I never get tired of riddles, and I hope you don't, either. What do the following riddles have in common?

> Why did the judge wear a catcher's mitt?
> *The ball was in his court.*
> How come a pickle doesn't sweat?
> *It's cool as a cucumber.*
> Why did Jack the Ripper get rich?
> *He made a killing.*
> When does a tea bag tremble?
> *When it's in hot water.*

Yes, I know they're silly. But what else do they have in common? . . . OK, time's up! They all have clichés as punch lines.

It's raining clichés!

A cliché is a tired, worn-out expression that you've heard a million times, more or less. (It's pronounced "klee-SHAY," and it has an accent mark above the *e* because it comes from French.) Like leftover spaghetti, a cliché is great the first few times. But after a while, it loses its flavor (except in silly riddles).

There's nothing wrong with a colorful expression that uses words in an imaginative way (we call this a "figure of speech"). But the more colorful or lively or interesting an expression is, the more likely it will be loved, remembered, repeated, worn out, and finally reduced to a cliché. That's why some people say that the Bible and Shakespeare are full of clichés!

So what's the lesson here? Should all clichés be summarily executed? No. Let your ear be your guide. If a familiar old expression sounds just right and nothing else will do, fine. If it sounds tired and overused, be merciless. Off with its head!

There's no way to get rid of all clichés. It would take a roomful of Shakespeares to replace them with fresh expressions, and before long those would become clichés, too. But think of clichés as condiments, the familiar ketchup, mustard, and relish of language. A little goes a long way. (Whoops, another cliché.)

I'll bet you know a lot of clichés. Everybody does—that's how come they're clichés. Let's have some fun and test your cliché IQ. (Don't sweat. This quiz is as easy as pie.) Fill in the blanks by picking the correct words from the list on the right.

Blankety-blank

busy as a _____	tomb
clear as a _____	fiddle
cute as a _____	beet
dead as a _____	pancake
fit as a _____	rock
flat as a _____	doornail
free as a _____	fox
fresh as a _____	bell
happy as a _____	kite
hard as a _____	fruitcake
high as a _____	bee
light as a _____	sheet
pretty as a _____	daisy
nutty as a _____	mule
quiet as a _____	bird
red as a _____	button
sharp as a _____	board
sly as a _____	tack
stiff as a _____	picture
stubborn as a _____	clam
white as a _____	feather

Isn't it fun to make fun of clichés? Here are more of these secondhand expressions. Use them if you must, but sparingly. The tired old things could stand a rest.

> **Back to the drawing board.** Back to *Roget's Thesaurus.*
>
> **Between a rock and a hard place.** Don't go there.
>
> **Bite the bullet.** Save your teeth.
>
> **Blanket of snow.** Sleep on it.
>
> **Blessing in disguise.** Not disguised well enough.
>
> **Boggles the mind.** You can be boggled now and then, but don't make a habit of it.
>
> **Bored to tears.** Bo-o-o-o-ring!
>
> **Bottom line.** Get off your bottom and find a better way to say it.
>
> **Broad daylight.** The sun has set on this one.
>
> **By leaps and bounds.** Leaping lizards!
>
> **Calm before the storm.** Tranquilizer, anyone?
>
> **Can of worms.** Don't open it too often.
>
> **Crystal clear.** Of quartz not!
>
> **Cut to the chase.** Cut it out.
>
> **Cutting edge.** Not sharp enough.
>
> **Easier said than done.** What isn't?
>
> **Eat like a pig.** Call Weight Watchers.
>
> **Fall through the cracks.** Leave it there.
>
> **Food for thought.** Go on a diet.

Fools rush in. And when they get there, they use clichés.

Get the show on the road. It's curtains for this expression.

Green with envy. Jealousy will get you nowhere.

Grind to a halt. OK, you can use this maybe once a year.

Impenetrable fog. Clear your head.

In the nick of time. "Just in time" isn't good enough?

Innocent bystander. Oh, yeah? Has he taken a lie-detector test?

It goes without saying. Then don't say it.

Last but not least. If it's not least, then don't put it last.

Mass exodus. Drop the *mass*, unless you mean a crowd leaving St. Peter's.

Moment of truth. Why is it always bad news?

More than meets the eye. See your optometrist.

Narrow escape. Thinny thin.

Needle in a haystack. Ouch!

Nip it in the bud. Let's nip this one in the bud.

Only time will tell. Get a watch.

Pandora's box. Put a lid on it.

Piece of cake. Don't stuff yourself.

Play hardball. Three strikes and you're out.

Play it by ear. Let's not wear it out, except at the piano.

Push the envelope. Only if you're sorting letters.

Raining cats and dogs. Call the pound.

Scream bloody murder. Keep your voice down.

Seat of the pants. Don't wear them out.

Spinning your wheels. Not unless you're skateboarding.

Stick out like a sore thumb. Try an ice pack.

Take the bull by the horns. You first.

Tight ship. It's leaking.

Tip of the iceberg. Anyone for a cruise on the *Titanic*?

Tongue in cheek. Bite your tongue.

Tough act to follow. Get a new act.

24/7. Time out!

Up in the air. Come back down to earth.

What makes him tick. This needs a new battery.

World-class. No class.

Like fast food, clichés are convenient, plentiful, and hard to avoid. But on special occasions, when you want your writing to be more of a gourmet meal, try using your imagination instead. Here's one way to be original.

METAPHORS BE WITH YOU

We all love figures of speech, the colorful expressions that juggle words in an imaginative way. Just think how dull our lives would be without them.

The metaphor, the most common figure of speech, lets us use the language of one thing, like astronomy, to describe something else, say fashion. *The gown was a galaxy of sequins.*

Imagine that! With metaphors, imagination is the only limit. They give us about a zillion different ways (give or take) to describe something like a dress. Instead of astronomy, we could use the language of fire: *The gown was ablaze with sequins.* Or the language of water: *The gown was dripping with sequins.* Or magic: *The gown was an enchantment of sequins.*

But don't let your imagination run away with you. If you're using fire language to describe a dress, don't suddenly switch to water language. *The gown was ablaze with dripping sequins.* What's wrong with this picture? The two images (one blazing and one dripping) clash with each other. The result is a jumble that doesn't make sense. This is called a mixed metaphor.

Unless you're a stand-up comic and deliberately trying to sound ridiculous, don't mix your metaphors, especially if they're clichés. *The tip of the iceberg sticks out like a sore thumb.* Or, as Farmer McGregor might put it, *Don't count your chickens till the cows come home.*

I'm not saying you should never use two metaphors in a row. As long as your word pictures don't clash, be my guest. Here's an example: *Professor Snape ran a tight ship, but his students were plotting a mutiny.* In this case, two seafaring images make for smooth sailing.

CHAPTER 12

ONLINE SKATING
The Rules of the Road

h3y bro w@sup? r u goin 2 da party? cud I getta
    ride? ttyl :)

If you can read that, maybe you're spending too much time at the computer (lol)!

OK, we know that some of the writing we do online has a special language all its own. That's one of the reasons instant messages are so much fun. When trading news flashes with your best friend, you feel free to be creative with things like grammar and spelling and punctuation.

Go ahead and goof around with your pals. Just lose the goofy English when you write to grown-ups who may not get it or appreciate it, like an English teacher or a picky parent or someone considering you for a summer job.

The important thing is that you and the people in your address book understand each other. And guess what? That's the most important thing in any kind of writing, whether you do it with a laptop or a ballpoint pen or in Morse code. The audience you're writing to—a friend, a teacher, Uncle Herb in Milwaukee, the family you babysit for—determines how you write the message.

Yes, even an instant message.

Say your teacher gives you a homework assignment and doesn't mention when it's due. You might instant-message a friend: "wenzit do???" But if you IM the teacher (especially an English teacher!), the message should look very different: "When is it due?"

The lesson? Know your audience!

Like many kids, you probably write more IM's than e-mails right now. But as time goes by, you'll find yourself depending more and more on e-mail to communicate online. And you'll be writing not just to friends and relatives but to people who don't know you well.

You'll also be posting messages to blogs, bulletin boards, discussion groups, and other public forums read by total strangers. All they know about you is what they see on their screens. As far as they're concerned, you are what you write.

So here are two important things to keep in mind when you're writing online. First, the less familiar you are with the guy at the other end, the more careful you should be about what you say. Second, the more public the forum, the less goofy you should be with your English.

As I said, you'll be relying more and more on e-mail in the future, especially for messages that matter. Follow these ten rules when your e-mail should be its best.

1. Keep the reader in mind.

Think of the person you're writing to. That vomit joke might be perfect for a message to your disgusting brother, but Grandma might not appreciate it.

2. Use a helpful subject line.

A blank subject line, or one that just says "Hi," doesn't help the person who gets the message. The reader should be able to tell at a glance what your e-mail is about ("Summer job" or "Thanks for the check!"). And skip the hype ("An offer you can't refuse!!!"), or a stranger might mistake your message for spam.

3. Put the important stuff first.

If you have something important to say ("Don't look at the report card until I have a chance to explain"), say it right away. A lot of people just glance at the beginning of an e-mail, especially a long one, then save it to read later.

4. Watch your English.

When you want to look your best, pay attention to grammar, spelling, and punctuation. Good, clear English avoids misunderstandings and makes you look smart. Gorgeous, too!

5. Use both big and small letters.

Messages with both capital letters and small ones are easier to read. Big letters let readers know at a glance where sentences begin and which words are important. Don't be a shiftless writer. Use the Shift key once in a while.

6. Go easy on the cybertalk.

Skip the cute smileys and frownies, the witty abbreviations, and other Internet expressions if there's any chance that your reader won't appreciate them. This kind of creativity is wasted on people who don't get it.

7. Check your facts.

The Internet is full of misinformation, so be careful about what you pass on. If something sounds too good to be true, it probably is.

8. Be selective.

Are you sure the soccer coach wants to see all fifty of those elephant jokes? (I don't think so.) Send only the best ones, and only if you just know she'll die laughing. The same goes for anything else you're tempted to copy or forward. Be sure you have an appreciative audience, then pick out the best parts to send.

9. Remember your manners.

Small slights are magnified in e-mail, and offhand remarks can be taken the wrong way. When you're on your best behavior, you ask for something—you don't demand it. Use words like "please," "thank you," and "sorry." And don't pick your nose, either.

10. Read it again.

Look over your message once more before you click "Send." Make this a habit. What takes a teeny moment can save you from big embarrassment. Someday you'll thank me!

Some Technical Terms
and What They Mean

ABBREVIATION. A shortened form of a word or phrase, like *Dr.* for "Doctor" or *USA* for "United States of America." When it's not necessary to spell something out, you can use one or more letters to do the job.

ADJECTIVE. A word, like *beautiful* or *tall* or *gloomy*, that helps you describe something or someone: **beautiful** *princess*, **tall** *tower*, **gloomy** *castle*.

ADVERB. A word, like *secretly* or *bravely* or *quickly*, that helps you describe an action: **secretly** *climbed*, *fought* **bravely**, **quickly** *escaped*.

APOSTROPHE. A punctuation mark ' that's used to show ownership (**Betty's** *grades*), to combine two words into one (**aren't**), or to make a single letter plural (*all* **A's** *and* **B's**).

CLAUSE. A mini-sentence with its own subject and verb. A simple sentence might consist of only one clause. *Hillary sang.* More complicated sentences have several clauses. *Billie Joe learned / that Hillary sang / before Jesse appeared onstage.*

CLICHÉ. A tired, worn-out expression, like *can of worms* or *tip of the iceberg.* (The word is pronounced "klee-SHAY," and it has an accent mark above the *e.*)

COLON. A punctuation mark 𝆛 that can be used to introduce a statement, a series of things, a quotation, or instructions. It's an abrupt stop, almost like a period. Think of the colon as a traffic cop that pulls you over and warns you about travel conditions up ahead. *This is the situation: the bridge washed out and a Hummer fell in.*

COMMA. A punctuation mark 𝆕 that indicates a pause. If it were a road sign, it would be a yellow light, as opposed to a stop sign. It can be used to separate clauses (that is, mini-sentences) within a sentence, or items in a series.

CONJUNCTION. A connecting word. The telltale part of this term is "junction," because that's where a conjunction is found—at the junction where words or phrases or sentences are joined together. The most common conjunctions are *and, but,* and *or.*

CONSONANT. Generally, a letter with a "hard" sound: *b, c, d, f, g, h, j, k, l, m, n, p, q, r, s, t, v, w, x, y, z.*

Sometimes the consonants *w* and *y* act like vowels, which are letters with "soft" sounds: *Few boys own many cows.* And occasionally consonants (like the *b* in *comb* or the *h* in *hour*) are seen but not heard.

CONTRACTION. Two words combined into one, with an apostrophe showing where letters are missing. A contraction is usually made up of a verb plus *not* (for example, *do + not = don't*); a pronoun plus a verb (*they + are = they're*); or a noun plus a verb (*Bob + is = Bob's*). Don't confuse the last example with a possessive, a word that shows ownership (*Bob's* dog).

DASH. A mark of punctuation ▬ that's like a detour sign. It interrupts a sentence to insert another thought. Use one dash if the thought comes at the end of a sentence. *It was every girl's nightmare—acne.* Use a pair of dashes if the interruption comes in the middle. *The next step was obvious—a visit to the dermatologist—but what would her boyfriend think?*

EXCLAMATION POINT. A punctuation mark ! that shouts to get attention. *Whoa!* It's like the horn on your car. But don't honk too much. Save the exclamation point for really startling stuff.

FIGURE OF SPEECH. A colorful expression that uses words in an imaginative way. *Clark says Lois knows how to **push his buttons**.* When a figure of speech gets worn out, it becomes a cliché.

GRAMMAR. A system of rules for using words and

making them into sentences. Why have rules? Because they make it easier for us to communicate.

HYPHEN. A mark of punctuation ⚊ that looks like a stubby dash. It's used to combine two words into one (*self-conscious*), and to link parts of a long word, like *hu-mongous*, when it breaks off at the end of a line and continues on the next.

INFINITIVE. A verb in its simplest form (*sneeze*, for example). While the word *to* usually accompanies an infinitive (*to sneeze*), it's not part of the infinitive itself. So putting a word in between (*to loudly sneeze*) is fine, even if some grown-ups say otherwise.

ITALIC. The slanting print (*like this*) that's often used for emphasis (*Yikes!*) or for the titles of long works like books, movies, and plays (*The Wizard of Oz*). Italic letters may also be used to set apart something, like the examples in this book. *Sir Lancelot laid his sword at King Arthur's feet.*

METAPHOR. One of the most common figures of speech. A metaphor takes the language normally used for one thing (like weather) and applies it to something else (like food). *Rachel's dessert was a cloud of whipped cream.*

NOUN. A word for a person, place, or thing. A common noun starts with a small letter (like *city* or *girl*); a proper noun starts with a capital letter (like *Chattanooga* or *Alexis*).

142

PARENTHESES. Marks of punctuation ( ) that enclose a detour or interruption in your writing. You can use the detour (one like this, for example) to tuck information inside a sentence. (Or you can put a whole sentence, like this one, in parentheses.)

PERIOD. A punctuation mark ● that shows where an ordinary sentence (one that states something) ends. Think of it as a stop sign. The period is also used in some abbreviations, like *St.* for "Street" and *etc.* for "et cetera."

PHRASE. A group of related words, like *banana peel, spill the beans,* or *with fries.*

PLURAL. More than one; just one is singular. Plural nouns (as in *a dozen **berries***) usually have endings different from singular nouns (*one **berry***). And plural verbs (as in *they **run***) often have endings different from singular verbs (*he **runs***).

POSSESSIVE. A word (like *Alice's* or *parents'*) that shows ownership or belonging. All you need to make almost any word possessive is an apostrophe and the letter *s.* You use both of them together (*'s*) or the apostrophe alone, depending on the circumstances. ***Alice's** mom and dad were late for **parents'** day.*

PREPOSITION. A word (like *above, below, down, up, in, out*) that tells you the position of something in relation to something else. Memory aid: The word *preposition* includes "position."

PRONOUN. A word, like *he* or *it* or *they*, that can be used in place of a noun, like *Harry* or *goblet* or *Hufflepuffs.*

PUNCTUATION. The marks in writing, much like road signs, that direct the traffic of language. They work like stops, starts, pauses, and detours. Punctuation marks include the period, the comma, the semicolon, the colon, the question mark, the exclamation point, parentheses, the dash, the apostrophe, quotation marks, and the hyphen.

QUESTION MARK. The punctuation mark ❓ that follows a question. *Huh?*

QUOTATION MARKS. Punctuation marks " " that enclose spoken or quoted words. *"Ah, Butler,"* Artemis *said. "It's you."*

SEMICOLON. A punctuation mark ; for a stop that's less final than a period. It's like a flashing red light; it lets you drive on after a brief pause. You'll find the semicolon between clauses (or mini-sentences) within a sentence, and in complicated lists.

SENTENCE. A word or group of words that expresses a complete thought. In writing, it begins with a capital letter and ends with a period, question mark, or exclamation point. Most sentences have a subject and a verb, but not all. Sometimes the subject or verb is hidden.

SINGULAR. Only one; more than one is plural. A singular noun (like *Popeye*) or pronoun (like *he*) or verb (like *is*) refers to a single person or thing. *Popeye is what he is.* (Or, as Popeye would say, "*I yam what I yam.*")

SUBJECT. Who or what is doing whatever is being done in a sentence. Subjects can be nouns (*Bobby*), pronouns (*I*), or phrases (*Bobby and I*). *Bobby and I have braces.*

TENSE. How a verb tells time or says when an action takes place. The basic tenses are present (*I **gargle***), past (*I **gargled***), and future (*I **will gargle***).

VERB. An action word. It tells you what's going on in a sentence. *She **sells** seashells.*

VOWEL. A letter with a "soft" sound: *a, e, i, o, u.* A letter with a "hard" sound is a consonant. Sometimes the vowels *u* and *eu* sound "hard" (as in *university* and *European*), and sometimes the consonants *w* and *y* sound "soft" (as in *dew* and *eye*).